THE BEST OF INDIVIDUAL COUNSELING

Activities For Use In Individual Counseling

Written by:

Madeleine Brehm
Wanda Cook
Kathie Guild
Pamela Hudgins
Susan Jelleberg
Arden Martenz
Melissa Richards
Marianne Vandawalker
Pat Vargas
Debra Wosnik

THE BEST OF INDIVIDUAL COUNSELING

Graphic Design: Cameon Funk

10-DIGIT ISBN: 1-57543-159-9
13-DIGIT ISBN: 978-1-57543-159-8

Published by mar*co products, inc.
1443 Old York Road
Warminster, PA 18974
1-800-448-2197
www.marcoproducts.com

PRINTED IN THE U.S.A.

TABLE OF CONTENTS/ TOPICAL REFERENCE

TABLE OF CONTENTS/ TOPICAL REFERENCE

TABLE OF CONTENTS/ TOPICAL REFERENCE

TABLE OF CONTENTS/ TOPICAL REFERENCE

TABLE OF CONTENTS/ TOPICAL REFERENCE

TABLE OF CONTENTS/ TOPICAL REFERENCE

INTRODUCTION

There's an ongoing, undeniable need for individual counseling. No matter how many groups counselors advise, classroom programs they conduct, or meetings they attend, there will always be students who require individual attention.

Although each counselor uses special techniques when working with individuals, we compiled this book with the realization that counselors are always looking for ideas that will enhance their work with students. Any one of the contributors has the experience and expertise to author such a publication, but Mar*co wanted something unique. Consequently, each of these published authors selected a few of the most effective techniques she uses in individual counseling. This book includes those techniques.

Instructions For Using The CD

The CD found on the inside back cover provides ADOBE® PDF files of each lesson's reproducible pages.

System requirements to open PDF (.pdf) files:

Adobe Reader® 5.0 or newer (compatible with Windows 2000® or newer or Mac OS 9.0® or newer).

For some of the pages, both color and and black and white versions of the reproducible have been provided. For example: *019_Ind Counseling.pdf* is the same as the black and white version of page 19 in the book and *019 color_Ind Counseling.pdf* provides a color version of the same page.

These files cannot be modified/edited.

A Note From Madeleine Brehm

Elementary school counseling has been my passion for the past 25 years. Its value is evidenced by its ability to reach children and meet their needs in a personal manner. Watching children experience life and helping guide them brings me unbelievable joy. The lessons I've chosen to share are aimed at creating the possibility of a fulfilling life. I believe this to be an important goal, because a personal history of successes and responsibility will enable our students to be resourceful no matter what life hands them.

Madeleine Brehm is a counselor in Texas. She is the author of *Get Rid Of The Hurt*, published by Mar*co Products.

PLAYING FOR A COMPLIMENT

Purpose:

To have the student improve social skills by giving and receiving compliments

Suggested Students:

Students with ADD/ADHD and students who have inadequate social skills

Grades 2–5

Materials Needed:

For The Leader:
- ☐ Single-hole punch
- ☐ Several 3" x 5" index cards
- ☐ Any game two people can play

For The Student:

None

Activity:

Give the student a 3" x 5" index card and take a card yourself.

Explain that the goal for this lesson is to see how many compliments the student can give while playing a 30-minute game with the leader. Each time the student gives a compliment, the leader will punch a hole in the student's index card. When the leader gives a compliment, the student punches a hole in the leader's index card. (*Note:* Have extra index cards on hand.)

Practice before the game starts to be sure the student understands what a compliment sounds like. For example:

- You play this game well.
- You're good at passing out the cards.
- You're good at passing out the game chips.
- Nice try!
- Good game!

- That was a good move.
- Thanks for not skipping my turn.
- You think before you move.
- Good strategy!
- You're a good helper.
- You put the game away neatly.
- I won, but you played a good game!
- I like playing this game with you.

Checkers, pick-up sticks, cards, and other games help a student practice playing fair, taking turns, sharing, and learning how to win or lose in a sportsmanlike manner.

Begin the game. Punch a hole in the student's card each time he/she gives a compliment. Remind the student to punch your card when you give a compliment.

After the allotted time has elapsed, have the student count the holes on his/her index card to determine the number of compliments he/she gave. Counting the number of holes is a great self-evaluation technique, and giving and receiving compliments is a true lifelong skill.

During the game, ask how the student feels about giving and receiving compliments. Explain that being aware of the world and complimenting others is a great skill.

Conclusion:

Remind the student of the importance of acknowledging a compliment by saying "Thank you."

PREPARE FOR TESTING DAY

Purpose:

To remind the student of the important skills test preparation requires

Suggested Students:

Students referred because of test anxiety

Grades 3–5

Materials Needed:

For The Leader:
None

For The Student:
☐ Copy of *Prepare For Testing Day* (page 19)

Activity:

Give the student a copy of *Prepare For Testing Day.*

Tell him/her to listen to what you say, then follow the directions on the sheet. Teach the student the importance of getting a good night's rest before a test by saying:

> ***Don't stay up late to watch your favorite show or come home late from visiting someone. If you're tired on testing day, you won't do your best.***

Have the student look at #1 on the activity sheet and put his/her head in his/her hands.

> Leader asks: ***What do you do the night before a test?***
>
> Student says: ***Sleep, sleep, sleep, sleep, sleep, sleep.***

Remind the student to go to bed on time. Stress the importance of eating a good breakfast by saying:

> ***Food gives you the energy you need to take the test. Even if you don't usually eat breakfast, eat something on the morning of the test. A piece of toast, glass of juice,***

nothing with a lot of sugar in it. Fruit to eat during a break in the test will be helpful, too.

Have the student look at #2 on the activity sheet and put his/her hand to his/her mouth.

Leader asks: ***What do you do the morning of the test?***

Student says: ***Eat, eat, eat, eat, eat, eat.***

Tell the student what to bring to the test by saying:

You need two number two pencils when taking a state-standardized test. The lead in a number two pencil is dark enough to make your marked answers easy to read.

Have the student look at #3 on the activity sheet and raise two fingers on each hand.

Leader asks: ***What do you take to the test?***

Student says: ***Two number twos! Two number twos!***

Teach the student to do his/her best by saying:

You must take your time during the test. Don't rush. Listening to all the directions is very important. Read the questions and possible answer choices three times. This will help you understand what the question is asking and is not asking. Take your time and do your best. This is not a race.

Have the student look at #4 on the activity sheet, raise both hands as if telling someone to stop, and rock his/her hands from side to side.

Leader asks: ***What speed do you use during a test?***

Student says: ***Not too fast and not too slow. Medium speed is the way to go.***

Teach the student about a positive attitude by saying:

Having a positive attitude will help you do well on the test. An "I don't care" attitude will hurt your testing score.

A sloppy and careless attitude will not help you do well on a test. Think positive thoughts. Say "I'm a great reader" or "I'm a great math student" or "I do well on tests."

Have the student look at #5 on the activity sheet and raise his/her hands in the air.

Leader asks: ***What do you say to yourself during the test?***

Student says. ***I can do this. I can do this. I can take this test. Yes, I can do this. I can do this. I can take this test, yes!***

Recite the activity sheet several times, having the student share the meaning behind each verse. Say:

In order for you to have a good attitude about taking a test, your brain needs to hear a positive message.

Conclusion:

Encourage the student to review the activity sheet before each test. If necessary, have the student come for a session with you before a test.

PREPARE FOR TESTING DAY

Leader asks: ***What do you do the night before the test?***
Student says: ***Sleep, sleep, sleep, sleep, sleep, sleep.***

Leader asks: ***What do you do the morning of the test?***
Student says: ***Eat, eat, eat, eat, eat, eat.***

Leader asks: ***What do you take to the test?***
Student says: ***Two number twos! Two number twos!***

Leader asks: ***What speed do you use during a test?***
Student says: ***Not too fast and not too slow. Medium speed is the way to go.***

Leader asks: ***What do you say to yourself during the test?***
Student says: ***I can do this. I can do this. I can take this test. Yes, I can do this. I can do this. I can take this test, yes!***

FRIENDSHIP—I AM NOT YOUR PUPPET

Purpose:

To help the student learn to speak up to a friend

Suggested Students:

Students referred because of low self-esteem

Grades 2–6

Materials:

For The Leader:
- ☐ Puppets or stuffed animals
- ☐ Hand mirror

For The Student:
None

Activity:

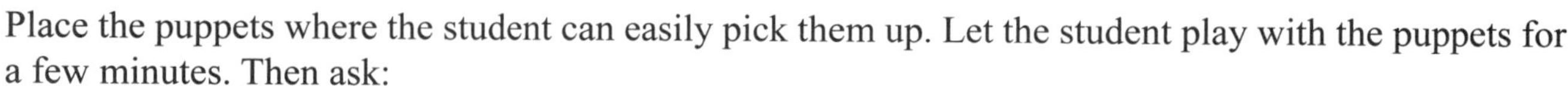

Place the puppets where the student can easily pick them up. Let the student play with the puppets for a few minutes. Then ask:

> ***Can the puppets do anything on their own?***
>
> ***Can the puppets talk on their own?***
>
> ***Do the puppets have a say in what they can or can't do?***
>
> ***Are you a puppet?***
>
> ***Is someone pulling your strings to make you move a certain way, go where he or she wants you to go, or play only with people he or she chooses for you?***

Ask if the student has ever heard anyone say:

- Don't play with that person! I don't like him.
- Don't sit there. Sit with me.
- Stand in line with me, not them.
- If you play with them, I'm not going to be your friend.
- You played with them yesterday. You have to play with me now.
- You can't be in our group.
- The game is closed. No one else can play.
- Don't wear that!
- I'm your best friend.

Ask what other statements like these the student has heard.

Continue by asking:

You can control the puppet, but should someone control you?

Do you have room in your heart for more than one friend or more than one best friend?

Are you afraid you'll lose a friend if you speak up?

Does your friend threaten not to be your friend if you play with someone else?

Are you a puppet?

Can you choose your friends? Will you?

Then say:

This isn't easy, because we don't like making a friend feel bad. But sometimes a friend makes you feel bad, and you don't want to be a puppet on a string.

Tell the student he/she is going to practice taking control of a friendship and not being anyone's puppet.

To explain the importance of *how* something is said, tell the student:

Look your friend in the eye.

Stand up straight.

Speak so you can be heard. When you order a burger and fries, do you want to be heard? This is at least as important.

Practice speaking up by starting your sentence with an **I-Message:**

> *"I feel (tell your feeling) hurt when you tell me if I play with someone else, you won't be my friend."*
>
> *"I want to play with that friend and would like you to join us when you're ready."*

Walk away and join your other friend. You may have to do this several times before your friend realizes you are not a puppet and can't be controlled.

The friend you left may be mad and may not be your friend for a day or two. That's OK. A friend who can't share you may not really be your friend. He or she may just want to control you. Let him or her look for another puppet. Your puppet days are over.

Then ask:

What would you like to say to your friend?

Give the student the mirror to practice what he/she would like to say to the friend. Then say:

Practice responding to a friend's statements that limit your relationships with others. Look and sound strong and assertive. This is not easy. Practice every day. Use your words to bring out the best in you. Soon you'll say "Bye, puppet. Hello, strong me."

Conclusion:

Say:

A friend should bring out the best in you. A friend should want the best for you.

GIMME, GIMME, I WANT IT!

(*Note:* Presented before holidays or the student's birthday, this session can provide a relevant lesson about life.)

Purpose:

To create an awareness of the difference between *want* and *need*

Suggested Students:

Students referred because of always wanting to have their own way

Grades 3-6

Materials:

For The Leader:
- ☐ Paper
- ☐ Pencil

For The Student:
None

Activity:

At the top of the paper, make columns labeled *Want* and *Need*. Then say:

> ***A* want *is something you'd like to have. A* need *is something you have to have.***

Ask the student to name all the things he/she wants, then all the things he/she needs. List each response in the appropriate column.

Pick one item from the *Want* list. For example, suppose the student has expensive tennis shoes on the list. You could say:

> ***You want expensive tennis shoes. Do you need a pair that costs $100? Or would a $40 pair work?***
>
> ***How long do shoes last?*** (A couple of months, because you outgrow them, they get dirty, etc.)

If your parents agree you need new tennis shoes, do you need an expensive pair? Or do you just need a new pair?

Explain that some kids feel they have to have everything they see. The latest tennis shoes, videogame, electronic device, team jacket, and on and on. Sometimes these kids have very little patience. They don't want to wait for what they want and don't consider that their parents need to budget the money for it. Then ask:

Do you help your parents shop for the best price? (Brainstorm about where to shop for the best price.)

Do you know what a* budget *is? (A budget is the amount of money you have to spend on items you need.)

Do you know how much is in your parents' budget for shoes?

Write out a pretend budget:

Pretend your parents get paid	$3300.00 a month
Rent/house payment is	- 1100.00 a month
Water/gas/electricity (utilities)	- 600.00 a month
Food	- 450.00 a month
Car payment	- 900.00 a month
Total	$250.00 a month

Continue the lesson by asking:

How many people live in your house? How much money is left over? ($250.00)

That isn't a lot of money. Do you see that maybe you can't get those expensive tennis shoes because the money is not in the budget? What can you cut out of the budget? (Nothing. All the listed items are things the family needs.)

Next time your parents say you can't have something you want, think about the budget. Ask what you can do to earn money to buy the items you want.

Next time you want something, ask yourself, "Do I need this or do I want this?"

Conclusion:

Say:

Your parents have feelings, and they want the best for you. Don't whine when you don't get what you want. Think of all the things you have but don't need and about how you can share them.

KEEP YOUR WORD

Purpose:

To provide awareness that others will trust a student who keeps his/her word

Suggested Students:

Students referred as a result of not being responsible

Grades 2–5

Materials:

For The Leader:
- ☐ Picture of a bicycle (optional)

For The Student:
- ☐ Drawing paper
- ☐ Pencil with eraser

Activity:

Give the student drawing paper and pencil. If you're using the bicycle picture, point out the spokes on the wheels.

Write *Integrity* in large letters on the paper. Explain that *integrity* means keeping promises. Then say:

> ***Draw a bicycle on your paper. Be sure the wheels have spokes.***
>
> ***A bicycle works great when the wheels have all their spokes.*** (Start erasing one spoke at a time.) ***But the bike won't work as well when some of the spokes are missing.***
>
> ***The same thing is true when we don't keep promises. When that happens, some of our spokes are missing and life doesn't work as well. We get into trouble. We get grounded. People don't trust us. We get upset. We lose friends.***

Brainstorm about times when life lacks integrity by asking:

> ***If you promise to do your homework and don't do it, are you keeping your word?*** (No. Have the student erase a spoke.)

If you say you're going to study and don't do it, do you have integrity? (No. Have the student erase a spoke.)

If you say you're going to feed your pet and don't do it, are you keeping your word? (No. Have the student erase a spoke.)

If you promise to be home on time and aren't, do you have integrity? (No. Have the student erase a spoke.)

If you promise not to hit and you hit someone, are you keeping your word? (No. Have the student erase a spoke.)

If you say you'll call someone and you don't call, do you have integrity? (No. Have the student erase a spoke.)

Tell the student to think about the times when he/she broke promises or didn't keep his/her word. Ask how many spokes the student thinks are missing from his/her life. Then ask:

How do you restore (get back) your integrity? (By keeping your word and promises.)

Honor your words. Just like the **Declaration of Independence** ***declares our freedom, declare that you'll do what you say you're going to do. Put those spokes back on your bike by honoring and keeping your word. Say:***

I'll do my homework. I'll turn it in when I get to class. (Have the student restore a spoke.)

I'll study 20 minutes for the test. I'll do it! (Have the student restore a spoke.)

I'll feed my pet as soon as I get home. I'll do it! (Have the student restore a spoke.)

Tell the student to keep track of how many times in one day he/she honors his/her word and keeps promises. Then say:

Keeping your word is a trait you should honor and restore every day.

Conclusion:

Set a time for the student to tell you how well he/she kept his/her word. Discuss, at this time, what the student must do to restore integrity lost when his/her promises weren't kept.

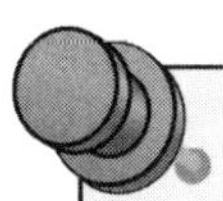

A Note From Wanda Cook

My name is Wanda S. Cook. I am a fifth-grade counselor at Ruby Reed Academy for Engineering in Houston, Texas; an LPC intern, and the author of *Guidance for the Gourmet* (Mar*co Products). I am married to husband and friend Joseph, and have the distinct honor of being mother to two of the world's most amazing sons, Joseph Jr. and John-Michael.

As an experienced counselor, I've found that the problems faced by some of today's children appear to be more varied and more complex than those faced by children in the past. The individual lessons I've written address sensitive issues that, unfortunately, are more prevalent than any of us care to admit. When confronted with painful and difficult situations, young children look to adults for guidance and comfort.

My lessons give children a forum in which to acknowledge and discuss those secret sources of pain and provide adults with effective resources to help children navigate their personal troubled waters.

I RESPECTFULLY DISAGREE

Purpose:

To help students learn how to disagree with adults in a respectful manner

Suggested Students:

Students who have been referred for arguing with adults and students who feel an adult has falsely accused them

Grade Levels 4-6

Materials Needed:

For The Leader:

- ☐ Office referral or a statement from the adult involved
- ☐ Copy of *How To Disagree Respectfully* (page 30)

For The Student:

- ☐ Copy of *How To Disagree Respectfully* (page 30)

Activity:

Ask the student to define *respect* and *disrespect*. If the student is misguided assist with the definitions.

Have the student tell his/her version of the incident for which he/she was referred.

Read the office referral or statement from the adult involved in the incident to the student.

Ask the student what he/she wanted to convey to the adult before the situation got out of hand.

Give the student a copy of *How To Disagree Respectfully*. Review the handout with the student.

Reenact the conflict having the student play the role of the adult and the leader the role of the student.

Have the student point out things that the leader, who portrayed the student, said or did during the dramatization that was inappropriate referring to the *How To Disagree Respectfully* handout as a guide.

The leader and the student will switch roles and reenact the incident again. This time the leader will play the role of the adult and the student will play himself/herself.

Conclusion:

Conclude the lesson by arranging for the student and the adult involved in the incident for which the student was referred to meet. The student must agree to be respectful, to follow the rules discussed during his/her session, and agree to accept the adult's final decision.

HOW TO
DISAGREE
RESPECTFULLY
Stay calm and listen to
the adult's accusation
When the time is
right ask to speak
Use a calm voice and
state your view
Wait for the adult to respond
Pay attention when the adult is speaking
Do not interrupt even if you disagree
Read the adult's body language
Decide if it is the right time
to continue the discussion or
to remain silent
Follow the adult's instructions

FRIENDSHIP SHOULDN'T HURT

Purpose:

To help students recognize the characteristics of healthy friendships

Suggested Students:

Students who have been referred for having frequent conflicts with friends

Grade Levels 4-6

Materials Needed:

For The Leader:
- ☐ Copy of *Good Friend Checklist* (page 33)
- ☐ Copy of *Good Friend Contract* (page 34)
- ☐ Copy of *End of Friendship Contract* (page 34)
- ☐ Yarn
- ☐ Scissors

For The Student:
- ☐ Copy of *Good Friend Checklist* (page 33)
- ☐ Piece of paper
- ☐ Pencil or marker

Activity:

Discuss the attributes of a good friend (friends are polite, helpful, supportive, trusting, protective, encouraging, giving, and forgiving).

Give the student a piece of paper and a pencil or marker. Ask the student to make a list of his/her friends.

Ask the student to discuss the existing problem.

Give the student a copy of the *Good Friend Checklist*. Tell the student to complete the checklist.

Discuss the completed *Good Friend Checklist* with the student.

Ask the student to consider whether his/her friends are truly friends.

Bring the disputing students to the meeting. When all parties are together, discuss the qualities of a good friend using the *Good Friend Checklist* as a guide. (*Note:* The purpose of meeting with the other students at this time is to inform them that an adult is aware of the situation. In the cases at my school, this seems to curtail a lot of the catty behavior.)

Help the students decide if they want to be friends. If they agree to be friends they must sign the *Good Friend Contract*. If they decide not to be friends, they must sign the *End Of Friendship Contract.*

Conclusion:

This activity may be done with the students at the meeting or at a follow-up session. Have the student bring a friend to make friendship bracelets by following these instructions:

> Cut three pieces of yarn six to seven inches in length. Tie a knot leaving approximately ½ inch of the yarn free at one end. Braid the three pieces of yarn long enough to fit over the wrist of the student. Knot the yarn at the other end leaving approximately ½ inches of yarn. Place the bracelet on the wrist of the friend and tie the ends together. The friends will make one bracelet each. (The length of the yarn may need adjusting according to the size of the student's wrist.)

GOOD FRIEND CHECKLIST

X = Always
S = Sometimes
O = Never

FRIENDS	POLITE	HELPFUL	SUPPORTIVE	TRUSTING	GIVING	FORGIVING
Example: Abigail	x	x	x	x	x	x

GOOD FRIEND CONTRACT

I ________________________________ agree to be a kind, helpful, supportive, trusting, giving, and forgiving friend to ________________________________. I will work hard not to do or say anything hurtful. If I hurt my friend, I will apologize.

Signature ______________________

Date _________________________

END OF FRIENDSHIP CONTRACT

I ________________________________ have decided that ______________________________ and I cannot be friends. I agree not to say or do hurtful things. I agree to stay out of his/her space. If I do or say anything hurtful, I will apologize.

Signature ______________________

Date _________________________

HE SAID ... SHE SAID ...

Purpose:

To help students understand the devastating effect of harmful words

Suggested Students:

Students who are victims of vicious gossip and nasty rumors

Grade Levels 4-6

Materials Needed:

For The Leader:

☐ Copy of *How Rumors And Gossip Are Spread* (page 37)
☐ List of school rules

For The Student:

☐ Copy of *How Rumors And Gossip Are Spread* (page 37)

Activity:

Ask the student to state the rumor being spread by students.

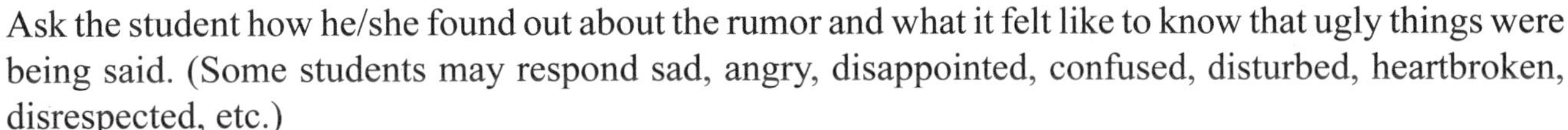

Ask the student how he/she found out about the rumor and what it felt like to know that ugly things were being said. (Some students may respond sad, angry, disappointed, confused, disturbed, heartbroken, disrespected, etc.)

Ask the victim to describe his/her relationship to those who started the rumors and why he/she feels he/she was chosen to be the victim.

Help the victim understand why others gossip and spread rumors. (Some of the reasons are jealousy, boredom, power, low self-esteem, etc.)

Give the student a copy of *How Rumors And Gossip Are Spread*. Use the sheet to help the student understand how rumors and gossip are fueled.

Tell the victim not to threaten or retaliate because of the rumors.

Have the person or persons spreading the rumor join the meeting to find out the origin of the problem, to discuss the school's rules, and to review *How Rumors And Gossip Are Spread.* Also discuss the harmful effects of gossiping.

If the problem persists, inform the principal and schedule a conference with the parents of those involved.

Schedule several follow up sessions to work on the victim's self esteem.

Conclusion:

Help the students start a Good News Club. The students in the club will get together and make a list of all the good things that they hear about others. The group could announce the good news during the morning announcements or create a newsletter or poster to share the good news. The newsletter or poster should be posted in a special place each week for all to see. (Students love this activity.)

HOW RUMORS AND GOSSIP ARE SPREAD

Gossiper

The Gossiper gives information to the runner or runners.

Runner(s)

The Runner(s) may decide to take the information directly to the victim or pass it on to an instigator.

Instigator

The instigator takes pleasure in passing the information on to the victim. It is not uncommon for the instigator to add statements to provoke action such as:

> "She said she wants to fight you."
> "He said that he can beat you."
> "I would not take that if I were you."

Victim

The victim will choose to retaliate, seek help, or internalize what has been said.

HANDS OFF MY STUFF!

Purpose:

To help the student break the habit of stealing

Suggested Students:

Students who have been referred for stealing

Grade Levels 3-6

Materials Needed:

For The Leader:
☐ Copy of *My Hands Off Plan* (page 40)

For The Student:
☐ Copy of *My Hands Off Plan* (page 40)

Activity:

Ask the student to name a toy, game, or personal item that he/she values.

Then ask the student how he/she would feel if someone took that item without permission.

Have the student tell what a person is doing when he/she takes something that is not his/hers. (Stealing. It is important to give the behavior a name.)

Ask the student the following questions, discussing the answers when necessary:

> ***How do you think the victim feels after discovering that his/her belongings were missing?***
>
> ***Do people usually steal when they are being watched or when they are not being watched? Why?***
>
> ***Have you ever taken things that did not belong to you? What was taken? Why?***

Think back to the first time you ever thought about taking something that did not belong to you. Tell me what you were feeling inside just before you took the item.

Was there something deep within you that told you not to steal? Did you listen to your inner voice?

What happened the next time you decided to take something? Did something tell you not to do it?

Did it become easier to take things after you ignored the helping voice inside over and over?

Explain that human beings have a built-in system inside that tells them when they are doing right or wrong. If they insist on not listening, the helping voice will gradually go away.

Taking things that do not belong to us is wrong and when wrong is done there are consequences. Some of the social consequences of stealing are: lack of trust; being blamed each time something is missing; being avoided.

Give the student a copy of *My Hands Off Plan*. Share the strategies from the plan with the student.

Conclusion:

Set up a reward system with the student using the *My Hands Off Plan*. Allow the student to help devise the reward system. Ask the student to name other adults whom he/she would like to join in the celebration. (Reward the student with stickers, game time, a healthy snack, a high-five, a pat on the back, a certificate, or a special phone call home.)

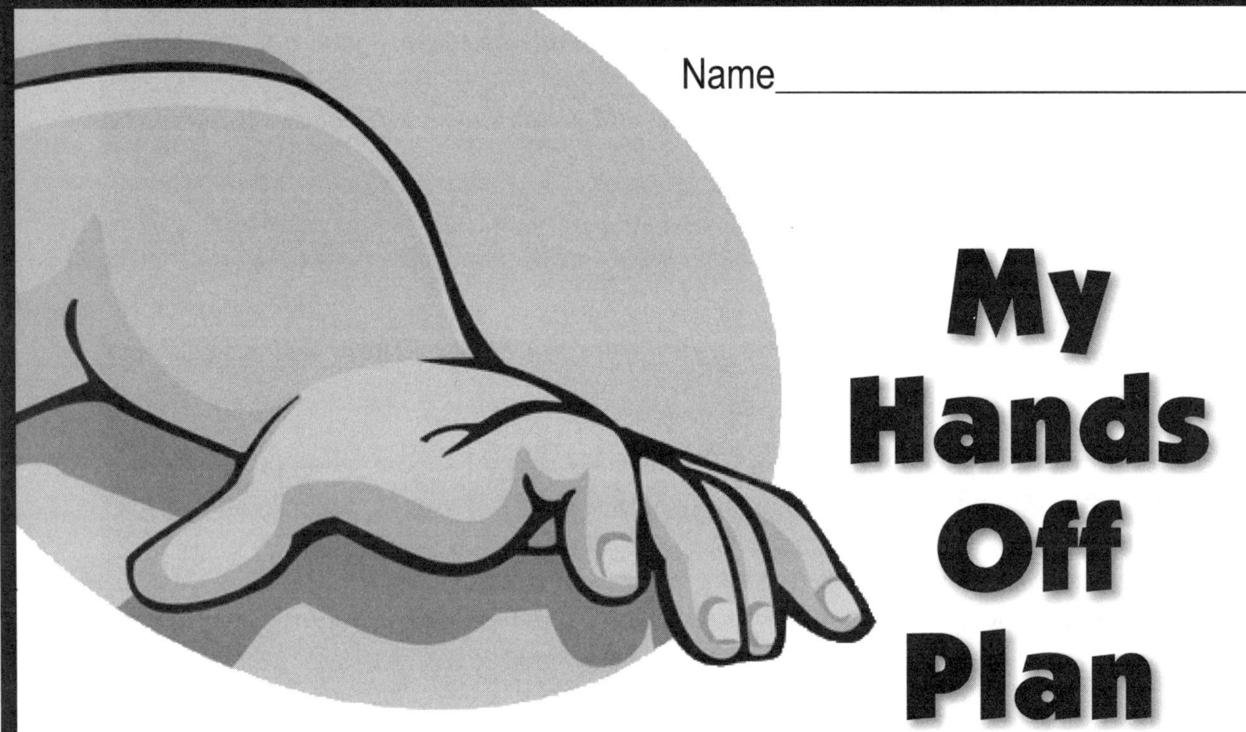

Name______________________

My Hands Off Plan

When I get the urge to steal, I will:

Tell myself that it's the wrong thing to do.

Listen to the helping voice inside.

Think about the consequences.

Walk away from the thing I want to take.

Find something fun to do with my hands.

Celebrate my good choice.

Color in a star each time you do what is right.

ELIMINATING SELF-DESTRUCTIVE BEHAVIORS

Purpose:

To help the student who relieves stress by causing physical harm to him/herself

Suggested Students:

Students who have been referred for cutting or other forms of self-mutilation

Grade Levels 5-6

Materials Needed:

For The Leader:

- ☐ Bubble wrap, stress ball, an orange, beads, string, paper, bowl of cool water (to be used with *Ten Things To Do Instead Of Cutting*)
- ☐ Copy of *Ten Things To Do Instead Of Cutting* (page 43)

For The Student:

- ☐ Spiral notebook, construction paper, markers, stickers, glue
- ☐ Copy of *Ten Things To Do Instead Of Cutting* (page 43)

Activity:

Help the student relax. Ensure the student that you are there to help and not judge.

Ask the student why he/she thinks he/she was asked to visit with you. After the student responds, say:

> ***You are here because someone who cares about you thinks that you are a cutter.*** (It is important to name the behavior.)
>
> ***Is this true?*** (Listen carefully to the answer. Watch the student's body language.)

When asking the student these questions, use good attending behavior. Be patient. This is a very sensitive topic. Some students may deny that the behavior exists initially because of fear and shame.

If the student's answer is *yes*, ask to see the student's scars. Then ask the student the following questions:

Whom do you cut with?

What do you use?

When was the last time you did it?

Where do you do it?

Why do you do it? (Most cutters will tell you that the behavior makes them feel better and gives them an odd sense of relief.)

Help the student understand that self-destructive behaviors usually derive from pain or conflict within and create bigger problems.

Review *Ten Things To Do Instead Of Cutting* with the student. As each suggestion is reviewed, have the student experience squeezing the stress ball, using the bubble wrap, tearing strips of paper, placing his/her hands in a bowl of cool water, peeling an orange, giving him/herself a hand massage, and stringing beads. Explain that these actions will help to deter the student from cutting when the urge overwhelms him/her.

Inform the student that part of the helping process is to involve others who care. This means contacting the school nurse, the student's parents or guardians, and the school principal.

Determine if you think the student needs to seek the help of an outside professional and, if so, work closely with the professional to help the student in the school setting.

(*Note:* If the student denies that he/she is a cutter, discuss the situation with the school nurse and ask her to check for scars. Contact the student's parents and the principal immediately if scars are found.

Conclusion:

Help the student create a personalized diary out of the spiral notebook and any available art supplies. The diary will help the student to identify triggers and possibly help identify destructive patterns the student may not be aware of. A diary is also an excellent tool for stress relief and self-expression.

10 THINGS TO DO INSTEAD OF CUTTING

1. Squeeze a stress ball until the urge disappears
2. Pop the air bubbles on the bubble wrap
3. Tear paper into tiny strips
4. Give yourself a firm pinch
5. Hold yourself tightly
6. Text or email a safe friend
7. Soak your hands in a bowl of cool water
8. Peel an orange
9. Give yourself a hand massage
10. String colorful beads

COPING WITH BODY IMAGES

Purpose:

To help those students who have difficulty with self-acceptance

Suggested Students:

Students who hate the way they look

Grade Levels 5-6

Materials Needed:

For The Leader:
- ☐ Bouquet of fresh flowers
- ☐ 2 sheets of newspaper or 2 sheets of wax paper

For The Student:
- ☐ Book for pressing the flower

Activity:

Show the student a bouquet of fresh flowers and ask the student to describe the different types of flowers in the bouquet.

Point out that although each flower has different petals, stems, and fragrances, each is beautiful and special in its own way.

Relate that people, like the flowers, are different: some are short, tall, thick, thin, light, dark, young, old. Yet each, like a flower, is beautiful and special.

Ask the student what he/she likes about him/herself, then ask what the student wishes to change about him/herself.

Explain that changing things that make a person different takes away the person's uniqueness.

Say that people love different flowers for different reasons and accept everything about that flower. For example: People who love roses accept their thorns.

Explain that when a person learns to accept him/herself, he/she will accept everything about him/her, even the things he/she wants to change.

Tell the student that he/she is a special rose and should learn to love and accept him/herself and have reasonable expectations about his/her appearance.

Have the student learn the following:

I'm happy to be someone very special
Unique in every way that I can be.
Because I am someone very special,
I'll learn to love every part of me.

Tell the student to recite this statement every day.

Conclusion:

Allow the student to choose a special flower from the bouquet. Teach the student how to press the flower in a book by giving the following instructions:

Place the flower between two sheets of newspaper/wax paper and place it inside of a book for a week or so. Weigh the book down with a heavy object. Affix the pressed flower to a bookmark, frame it, or find some other way to enjoy it.

Tell the student that the flower will serve as a reminder that he/she is unique and special.

A Note From Kathie Guild

I use the following books, art projects, and learning games to address common school behaviors and teach social skills. I use them to work with individual students on a variety of issues. Teaching to different learning styles improves students` attention and retention, and the lessons may be broken down into smaller segments. Each of the lessons includes a take-home component as a visual reminder of the topic discussed.

Kathie Guild is a counselor in North Carolina and is the author of *Everyone Is Included, Froggy And Friends, Froggy And Friends II, More Froggy And Friends,* and *How To Stop Before You Pop.*

SELF-ESTEEM/POSITIVE AFFIRMATIONS

Purpose:

To illustrate how individual effort and personal responsibility contribute to positive self-esteem

Suggested Students:

Students referred because of anxiety and/or issues regarding self-worth and social skills

Grades K–3 Train Art Activities/K–5 Tape Activity

Materials Needed:

For The Leader:
Tape Activity (K-5):
- ☐ Masking tape

Optional Book:
- ☐ *The Little Engine That Could* by Watty Piper

For The Student:
Art Activity (K-3):
- ☐ Copy of *Find The Train That Is Different* (page 50)
- ☐ Copy of *Train Maze* (page 51)
- ☐ Pencil

Introduction:

If you're using the storybook, begin by reading *The Little Engine That Could* to the student.

Then say:

> ***When we're small, we begin to learn things that help us be independent. When we were learning to walk, we often fell, but we got up and tried again. The same thing happened when we learned to ride a bike without training wheels. When we keep trying until we can do something successfully, we demonstrate effort and determination.***

Continue the lesson by asking/saying:

> ***What have you learned to do by practicing over and over?***
>
> ***We sometimes tell ourselves to give up or not try. We may say things like, "I usually stink at this" or "I can't do anything."***
>
> ***Have you ever had those thoughts?***
>
> ***Do you think those thoughts would encourage you to try or encourage you to stop trying?***

Train Art Activities (K–3):

Give the student a copy of *Find The Train That Is Different*, *Train Maze,* and a pencil.

Have the student complete both worksheets. Then ask:

> ***Why were you able to find the train that was different and complete the maze?*** (The student could do the worksheets because he/she kept trying.)

Tape Activity (K–5):

Ask the student to stand facing a wall.

Have the student reach as high as he/she can with one arm, keeping feet flat on the floor and toes touching the baseboard. With the masking tape, mark the place on the wall that the student's longest finger touches.

Tell the student to relax and stretch, then to repeat the experiment and try harder.

Mark the student's second attempt. It will be higher than the first, simply because the student stretched and was able to reach a higher spot on the wall.

Discuss how this simple experiment shows that effort and determination make a difference.

Conclusion:

Remind the student not to give up when something doesn't work out the first time he/she tries.

FIND THE TRAIN THAT IS DIFFERENT

TRAIN MAZE

START

SELF-ESTEEM/POSITIVE AFFIRMATIONS

Purpose:

To help the student clarify feelings about him/herself and recognize that positive thoughts translate into positive feelings

Suggested Students:

Students referred because of anxiety and/or issues related to self-esteem and poor social skills

Grades K–5

Materials Needed:

For The Leader:

Magic Mirror Activity (K-5):

- ☐ *Mirror Pattern* (page 54)
- ☐ Cardstock
- ☐ Mirror poster board (found in craft stores)
- ☐ Scissors
- ☐ Glue
- ☐ Permanent markers
- ☐ Stickers

  or
- ☐ Hand mirror

Beach Ball Toss Activity (K-5):

- ☐ Inflatable beach ball
- ☐ Permanent markers

Optional Books:

- ☐ *I Want To Be Somebody New* by Robert Lopshire
- ☐ *Arthur's Nose* by Marc Brown
- ☐ *Arthur's Eyes* by Marc Brown

For The Student:

None

Preparation:

***Magic Mirror Activity*:** Obtain a hand mirror or make a mirror from the *Mirror Pattern*. To make the mirror, cut an oval out of the mirror poster board. Reproduce the *Mirror Pattern* on cardstock and cut it out. Glue the mirror oval to the mirror pattern. Decorate the mirror with markers and stickers.

Beach Ball Toss Activity: Blow up the beach ball and mark it with random *X*'s and *O*'s. Using the permanent marker, write comments such as: Name something you like about your face. Name something you do well. Name someone who makes you feel good. Name something you can do when you're having a bad day. Name a place you like to go. Name something that cheers you up. What's the best compliment you've ever received? Name something that makes you laugh. (See an illustration of a finished beach ball on the previous page.)

Introduction:

If you're including a storybook, begin by reading it aloud.

Then continue the lesson by saying:

> ***Thoughts and feelings go together. For example, when you're lost or having a test, you may worry (thought) and worrying can cause feelings of anxiety or fear. On the other hand, if you're looking forward to going on a trip or visiting a friend (thoughts), you feel excited and happy. The same thing is true when you think about yourself. We feel good about things we do well and not as good about things we don't do well. Today, we're going to focus on the things you do well or that you like about yourself, because concentrating on good thoughts produces good feelings.***

Magic Mirror Activity (K–5):

Have the student look into the Magic Mirror and say positive things about him/herself.

Beach Ball Toss Activity (K–5):

Toss the beach ball back and forth between you and the student. Whoever catches the beach ball must answer the comment nearest his/her right thumb. If the right thumb lands on an *X*, the person must kiss his/her own hand. If the right thumb lands on an *O,* the person must give him/herself a hug.

Ask the student how it felt to say positive things about him/herself.

Conclusion:

Discuss the importance of positive thoughts and positive self-talk.

MIRROR PATTERN

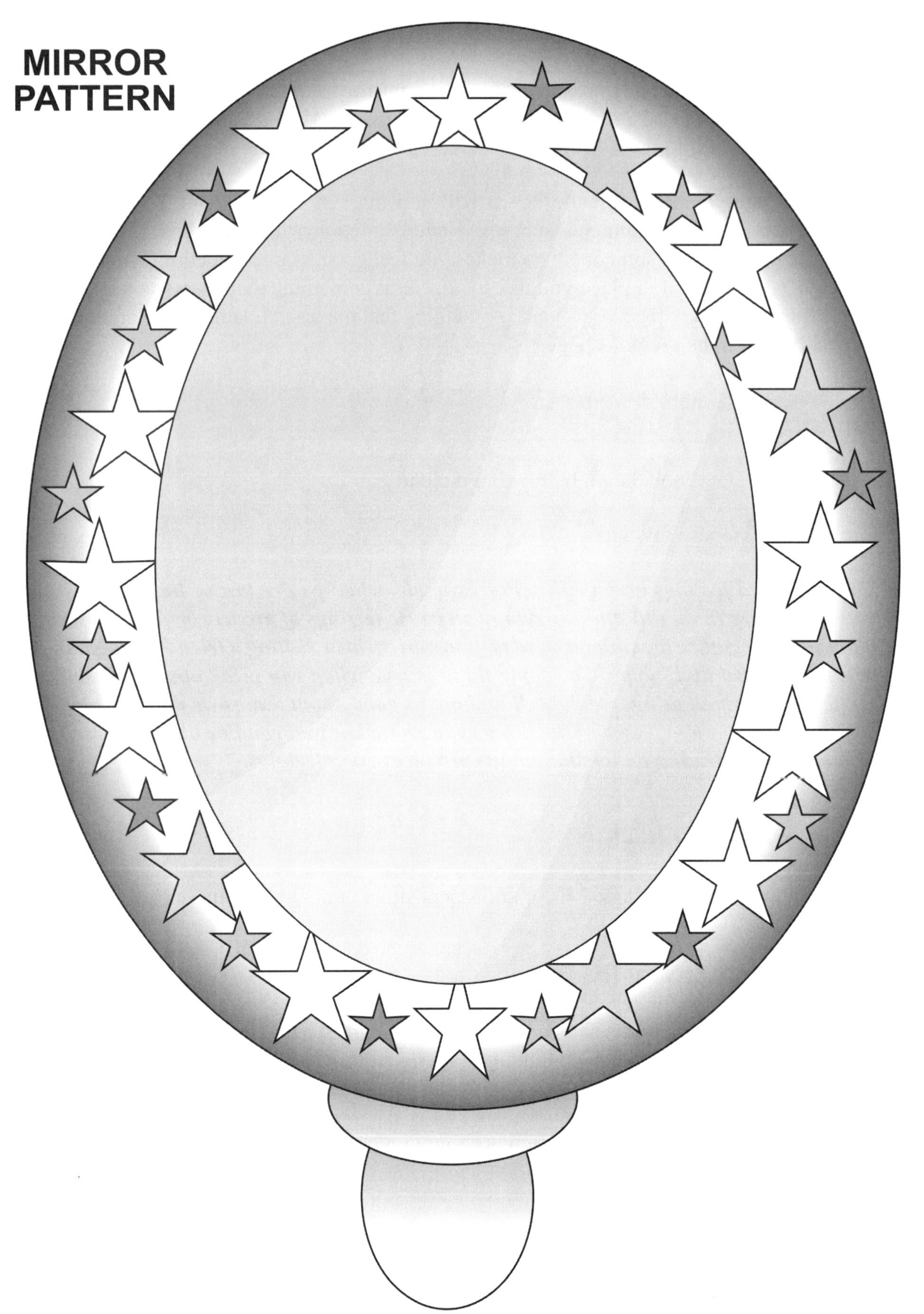

THE BEST OF INDIVIDUAL COUNSELING

WORRY AND ANXIETY

Purpose:

To help the student recognize that worrying thoughts create anxiety and can be habit-forming

To help the student understand he/she must begin thinking a new way in order to break the worrying habit

Suggested Students:

Students referred as a result of anxiety, excessive worrying, and/or stress

Grades K–5

Materials Needed:

For The Leader:

Stress Ball Activity (K-5):
- ☐ 12” round balloon
- ☐ Uncooked rice
- ☐ Empty water bottle
- ☐ Small paper/plastic cup
- ☐ Plastic bin for rice

Changing Habits Activity (K-5):
- ☐ Piece of unlined paper
- ☐ Purple, pink, black, brown, yellow, green, red, and blue markers

Optional Books:
- ☐ *Sam's Worries* by Maryann MacDonald
- ☐ *Wemberly Worried* by Kevin Henkes

For The Student:

None

Preparation:

***Stress Ball Activity*:**

Cover the bottom of the bin with uncooked rice.

Scoop the rice with the paper cup and pour about 2" of rice into the empty water bottle. Stretch the opening of the balloon to cover the mouth of the water bottle.

Turn the water bottle upside down. Shake and squeeze the bottle so the rice goes into the balloon.

When the balloon is filled with rice, remove it from the mouth of the water bottle. Tie off the end.

Changing Habits Activity:

Write the color words on the unlined paper. Write each word with a marker of a different color than the word. For example:

Write this word with this color marker:

red	purple
blue	pink
green	black
yellow	brown
brown	yellow
black	green
purple	red
pink	blue

Introduction:

If you're including a storybook, begin by reading it to the student.

Introduce the concept of *habits* by asking the student to name any habits he/she may have. Suggest such examples as nail biting, twirling hair, sleeping with TV on, and always sitting in a certain spot. Then ask:

Have you ever broken a habit or known someone who has?

Explain that we can break habits by using willpower or thinking in a new way.

Continue the lesson by asking/saying:

> ***Have you ever noticed that when you're busy, you sometimes forget to worry?***
>
> ***Staying busy is a good way to change the worrying habit. It's also important to change your thoughts. Replace your worries with a positive image or thought. It won't be easy at first. The worry might keep popping back into your brain. But with practice, positive thoughts and images will become a habit. It helps to start by practicing thinking positive thoughts when you're not worrying. This way, when you are worried, good memories and thoughts will crowd out the worries.***

Stress Ball Activity (K–5):

Prior to the activity make the stress ball. Or have the student help you make the stress ball. Then have the student practice using the stress ball. Give him/her the ball to keep and use at times when stress seems to be taking over his/her thoughts and actions.

Changing Habits Activity (K–5):

Show the student the sheet with the color words. Have him/her say out loud the colors used to write the words, not the words themselves. The student will have trouble doing this. That's because the words are common sight words, read out of habit.

After several attempts, the student will do the task correctly. Point out that this activity demonstrates that habits can be broken by practicing and concentrating on changing perceptions.

Explain that this idea can apply to the student's habit of worrying.

Conclusion:

Review the lesson's concepts by reminding the student to use the stress ball whenever he/she begins to feel anxious and that changing his/her perception of a situation can break his/her habit of worrying.

BOSSY OR IN CHARGE?

Purpose:

To help the student distinguish between being *bossy* and being *in charge*

Suggested Students:

Students referred because of poor social skills, friendship problems, or anger-control issues

Grades K–3

Materials Needed:

For The Leader:
In Charge/Bossy Statements Activity (K-3):
- ☐ *Bossy/In Charge Statements* reproduced on cardstock/heavyweight paper, cut apart, and placed in a container (page 62)
- ☐ Scissors
- ☐ Container

Optional Book:
- ☐ *Little Miss Bossy* by Roger Hargreaves

For The Student:
Bossy Boots Art Activity (K-3):
- ☐ Copy of *Design Your Own Bossy Boots* (page 60)
- ☐ Crayons or markers

Find The Boot That Is Different Activity (K-3):
- ☐ Copy of *Find The Boot That Is Different* (page 61)

Introduction:

If you're including the storybook, begin by reading it to the student.

Tell the student that he/she will be learning the difference between *being bossy* and *being in charge*. Then ask:

> ***Have you ever been told you were bossy? What were the circumstances?***
>
> ***Have you ever been in charge of something? What were the circumstances?***

Explain that someone who's in charge is like a boss and may give directions or commands. But someone who tells others what to do even though he/she isn't in charge or in a leadership position is being bossy.

Bossy Boots Art Activity (K–3):

Give the student a copy of *Design Your Own Bossy Boots* and crayons or markers. Allow time for the student to decorate and design the boots on the activity sheet.

Find The Boot That Is Different Activity (K–3):

Give the student a copy of *Find The Boot That Is Different*. Tell him/her to find the one boot that is different from the rest and circle it with a crayon/marker.

In Charge/Bossy Statements Activity (K–3):

Pull one paper at a time from the container. Read the statement on it aloud or have the student read it. Ask if the behavior is being bossy or in charge.

Conclusion:

Ask the student to tell you the difference between being bossy and being in charge.

DESIGN YOUR OWN BOSSY BOOTS

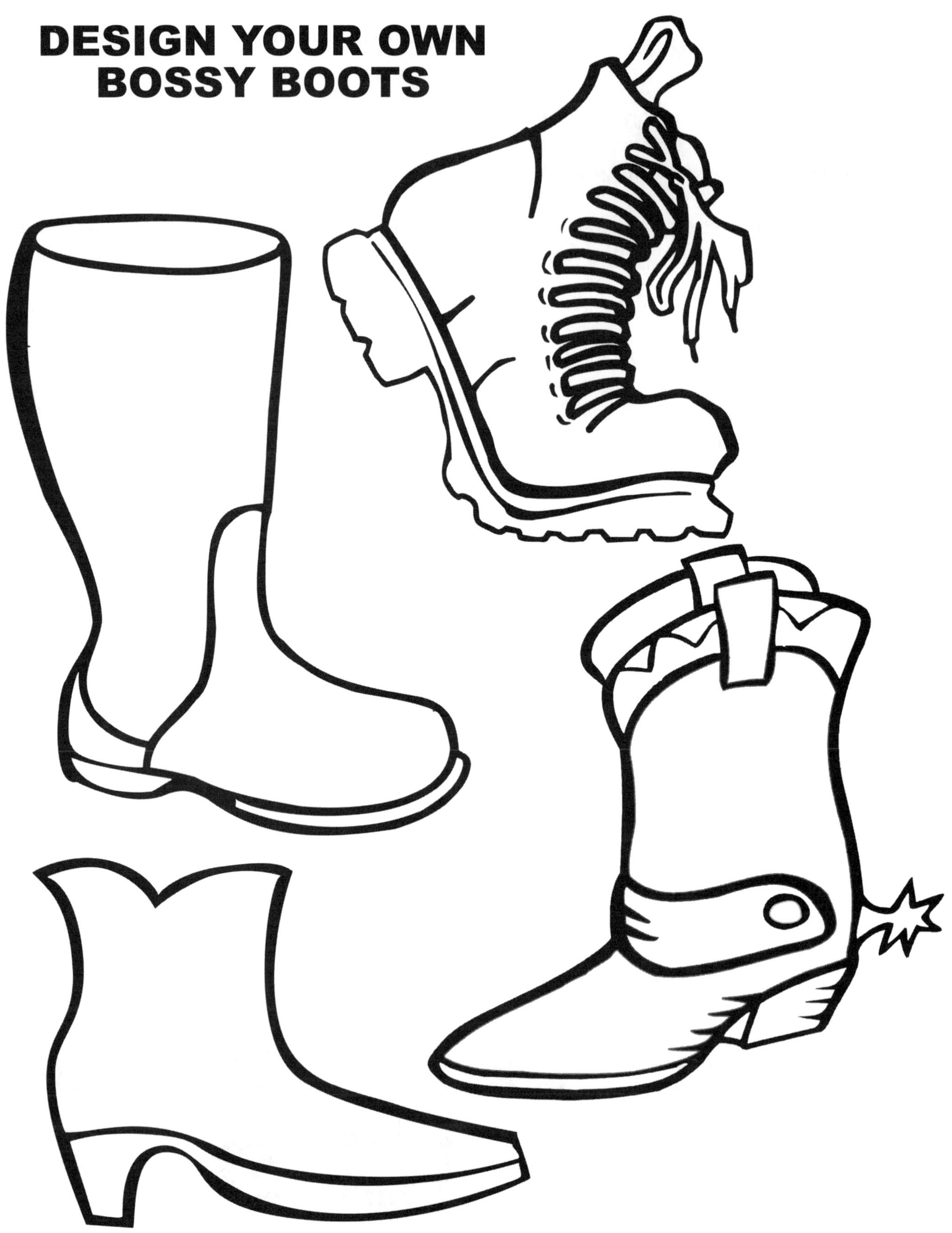

FIND THE BOOT THAT IS DIFFERENT

Directions: Find the boot that is in charge. Hint: It is different from the *Bossy Boots*.

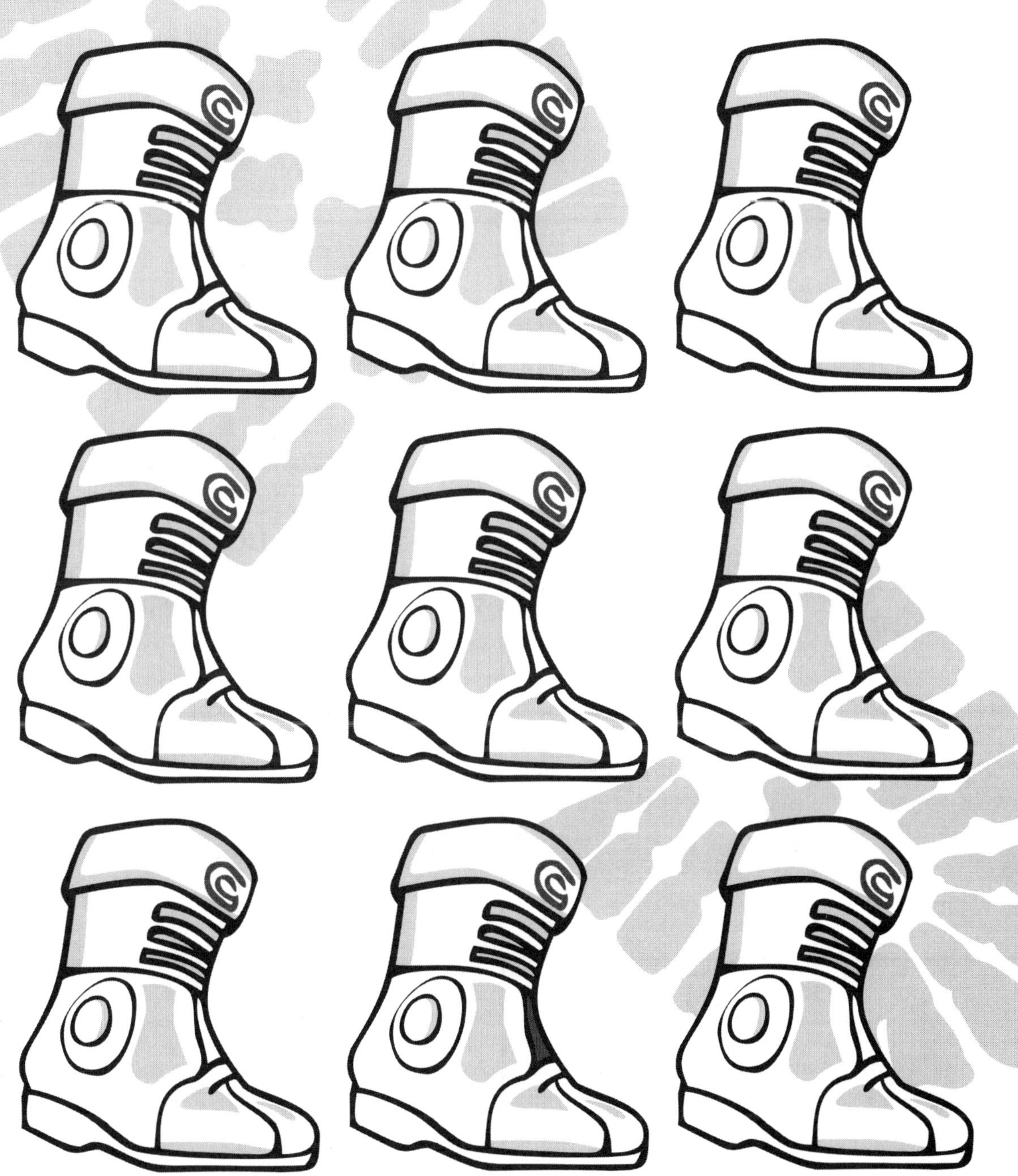

IN CHARGE/BOSSY STATEMENTS

You've been given the classroom job of table washer for the week. While wiping off the lunch table, you notice a student has left his napkin on the table. You ask the student to throw the napkin away so you can continue cleaning the table.	You've been given the classroom job of library helper. You announce that students must turn their books in since they are due back in the school library.
During a game of *four square,* you call out that you're team captain. Another student complains. But since you called it first, you don't back down.	At home, your older brother tells you to quiet down so he can finish his school report.
You're the line leader this week at school. While walking down the hall, you hear several students talking loudly. You stop the line, turn around, and say "Shhhh."	Your older sister tells you to get off the family computer so she can use it.
Your little brother keeps jumping up and down on your bed. When you tell him to stop, he says he's going to tell Mom on you.	You notice a student circling answers on a worksheet whose directions say to X the answers. You tell the student he's doing the worksheet wrong.
You're playing a pretend game at recess, and everyone has a part to play. Two of the students playing the pretend game tell you they've decided to give you a new role. You don't like the new part.	Some kids decide to play football. The kid who owns the football and his best friend appoint themselves captains and start choosing their teams. When some kids complain, the kid with the football says he gets to be the captain because it's his football.
During circle time, a student tells you to move because she can't see the teacher.	At the water fountain, a student tells you to hurry.

TATTLING OR REPORTING?

Purpose:

To help the student learn what should be reported to an adult and what should not

To have the student determine what would be *reporting* and what would be *squealing* (*tattling*) in a variety of situations

Suggested Students:

Students referred because of poor social skills and/or friendship issues

Grades K–3

Materials Needed:

For The Leader:
Introduction:
- ☐ Writing paper
- ☐ Pencil

Paper Pig Puppet Art Activity (K-3):
- ☐ 8½ x 11" drawing paper (optional)
- ☐ Crayons or markers (optional)

Squealing (Tattling) Or Reporting? Activity (K-3):
- ☐ Squeaky toy
- ☐ *Is It Squealing Or Reporting? Situations* reproduced on cardstock/heavyweight paper and cut apart (page 66)
- ☐ Scissors
- ☐ Container

Optional Book:
- ☐ *Don't Squeal Unless It's A Big Deal* by Jeanie Franz Ransom

For The Student:
Paper Pig Puppet Art Activity:
- ☐ 8½ x 11" drawing paper
- ☐ Crayons or markers

Squealing/Reporting Maze (K-3) :
- ☐ Copy of *Squealing/Reporting Maze* (page 68)
- ☐ Pencil

Preparation:

Paper Pig Puppet Art Activity: Optional: Make a sample pig puppet from the directions on page 67.

Put the cut-apart *Is It Squealing Or Reporting? Situations* into a container.

Introduction:

If you're using *Don't Squeal Unless It's A Big Deal*, begin by reading the book to the student.

Explain that it's often hard to tell the difference between *reporting* and *tattling*. Ask:

> ***Have you told something to an adult who said you were tattling?***
>
> ***Why do you think the adult responded this way?***

Tell the student the three basic rules about when something must be reported to an adult:

- A person or an animal is hurt or in danger.
- You are being hurt.
- Property is being destroyed or damaged.

Write down the rules for the student to take with him/her and refer to when needed.

Remind the student that if something doesn't fall into one of these three categories, telling an adult about it is *tattling* or *squealing*.

Explain that as the student gets older, adults will expect him/her to be able to handle situations falling outside these three rules.

Paper Pig Puppet Art Activity (K–3):

If you made a sample puppet before the session, show it to the student.

Give the student a piece of 8½ x 11" white copy paper to make his/her own paper pig puppet by following these directions (see page 67).

- Fold the paper into thirds lengthwise.
- Flip the paper over.
- Fold the paper in half.
- Fold the top edge back.
- Flip the paper over and fold the top edge back.

- The student may stick his/her fingers inside the pockets these folds create.
- The corners of the puppet's mouth may be bent to create teeth.
- Decorate the face with crayons or markers.

Squealing (Tattling) Or Reporting? Activity (K–3):

Give the student a squeaky toy and the paper pig puppet.

Choose (or have the student choose) a situation from the container. Read the card, then have the student decide if the situation it describes is squealing (tattling) or reporting and why. If the situation describes tattling, the student should squeeze the toy. If the situation describes reporting, the student should pick up the pig paper puppet and say "reporting."

Squealing/Reporting Maze (K–3):

Give the student a copy of the *Squealing/Reporting Maze* and a pencil. Have the student complete the maze, which reinforces the ideas presented during the lesson.

Conclusion:

Have the student repeat the three situations that describe reporting, not tattling.

- A person or an animal is hurt or in danger.
- I am being hurt.
- Property is being destroyed or damaged.

IS IT SQUEALING OR REPORTING? SITUATIONS

You are walking in the hall at school when a classmate passes you and rolls his eyes. Your feelings are hurt, so you decide to tell the teacher.	On the playground, you see two students breaking sticks into pieces and throwing them at other kids. You approach the students and tell them to stop. They say the sticks are too small to hurt anyone and they aren't throwing them far. You decide to tell the teacher.
A student sits so close to you during circle time that you feel squished. When you ask her to scoot over, she tells you she won't. You decide to tell the teacher.	At lunch, a student asks for some of your chips. You say she can't have any. She says, she's going to tell the teacher you won't share. Is the student tattling or reporting?
During morning work, you notice a student has forgotten to put his name on his paper. You remind him. The student tells you, "Mind your own beeswax." You tell the teacher.	When you go to sit down at lunch, a student tells you she's saving the seat and you'll have to sit somewhere else. You remind her that students aren't supposed to save seats. She argues and calls you mean. You tell the teacher.
Some kids are playing basketball at recess. Your team thinks the other team is cheating. You decide to tell the teacher.	At recess, you approach a group of kids who are standing and talking. You ask what they're doing and one of them tells you they're busy. You suspect they don't want you to join them. You tell the teacher they're leaving you out.
When you go to the boys bathroom, you see a boy from another class writing on the walls. You tell the custodian.	Two students sitting in the back of the bus leave their seats, slide under the seats of other students, and grab their legs. When you get off the bus, you tell the bus driver what you saw.
You pass a kindergarten student carrying a tray down the hall. The student spills food on the floor. You tell the front office.	In the bathroom, you notice students throwing wads of paper into the toilet, trying to stop it up. You tell the custodian.
Over the weekend, you went to a restaurant and a movie. You're telling the students at your table about it when a student from another table says you're making it all up. You tell the teacher.	You have a new haircut. Two students in your class tell you they liked your hair better the way it was before. You tell the teacher.

PAPER PIG PUPPET PATTERN

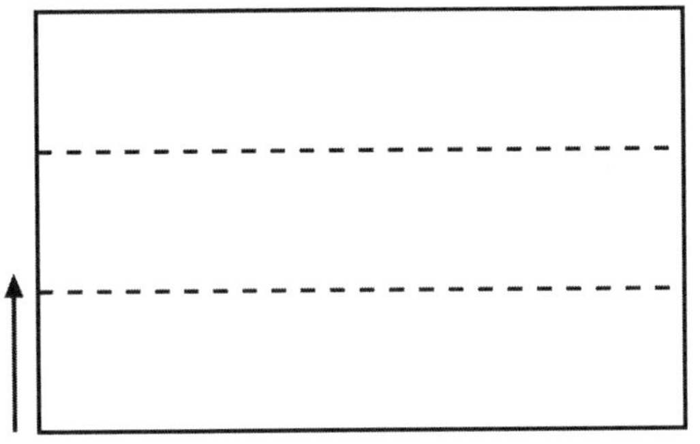

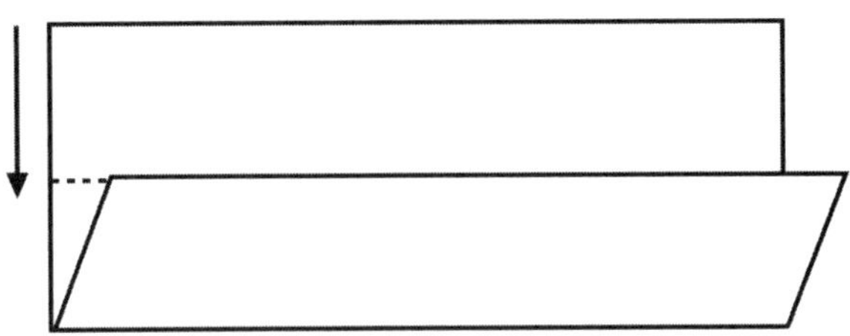

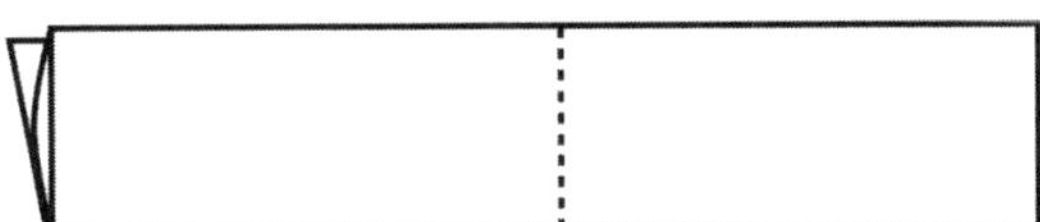

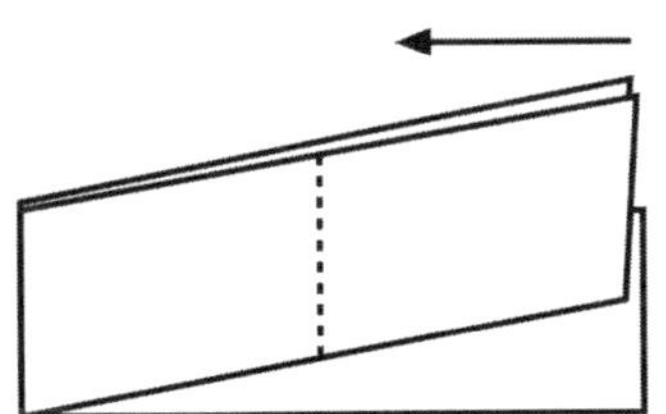

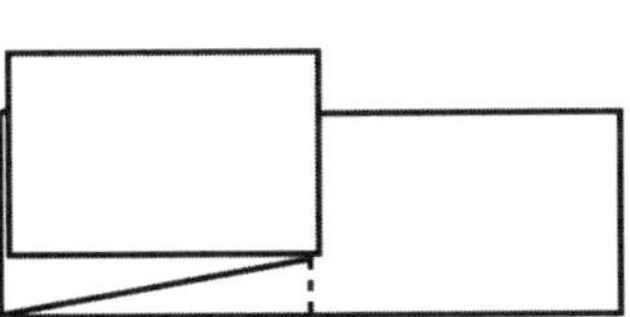

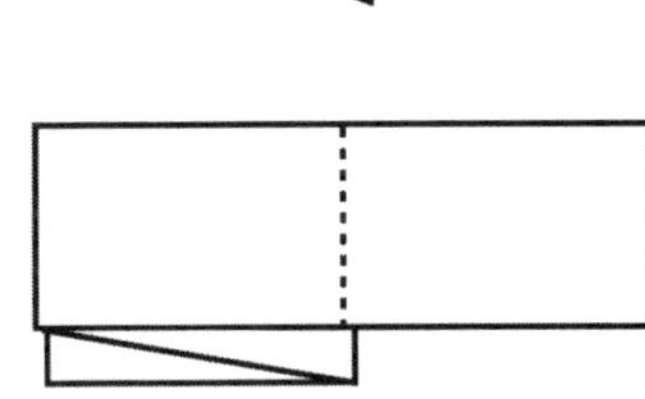

Give the student a piece of 8½ x 11" white copy paper to make his/her own paper pig puppet by following these directions.

- Fold the paper into thirds lengthwise.
- Flip the paper over.
- Fold the paper in half.
- Fold the top edge back.
- Flip the paper over and fold the top edge back.
- The student may stick his/her fingers inside the pockets these folds create.
- The corners of the puppet's mouth may be bent to create teeth.
- Decorate the face with crayons or markers.

SQUEALING/REPORTING MAZE

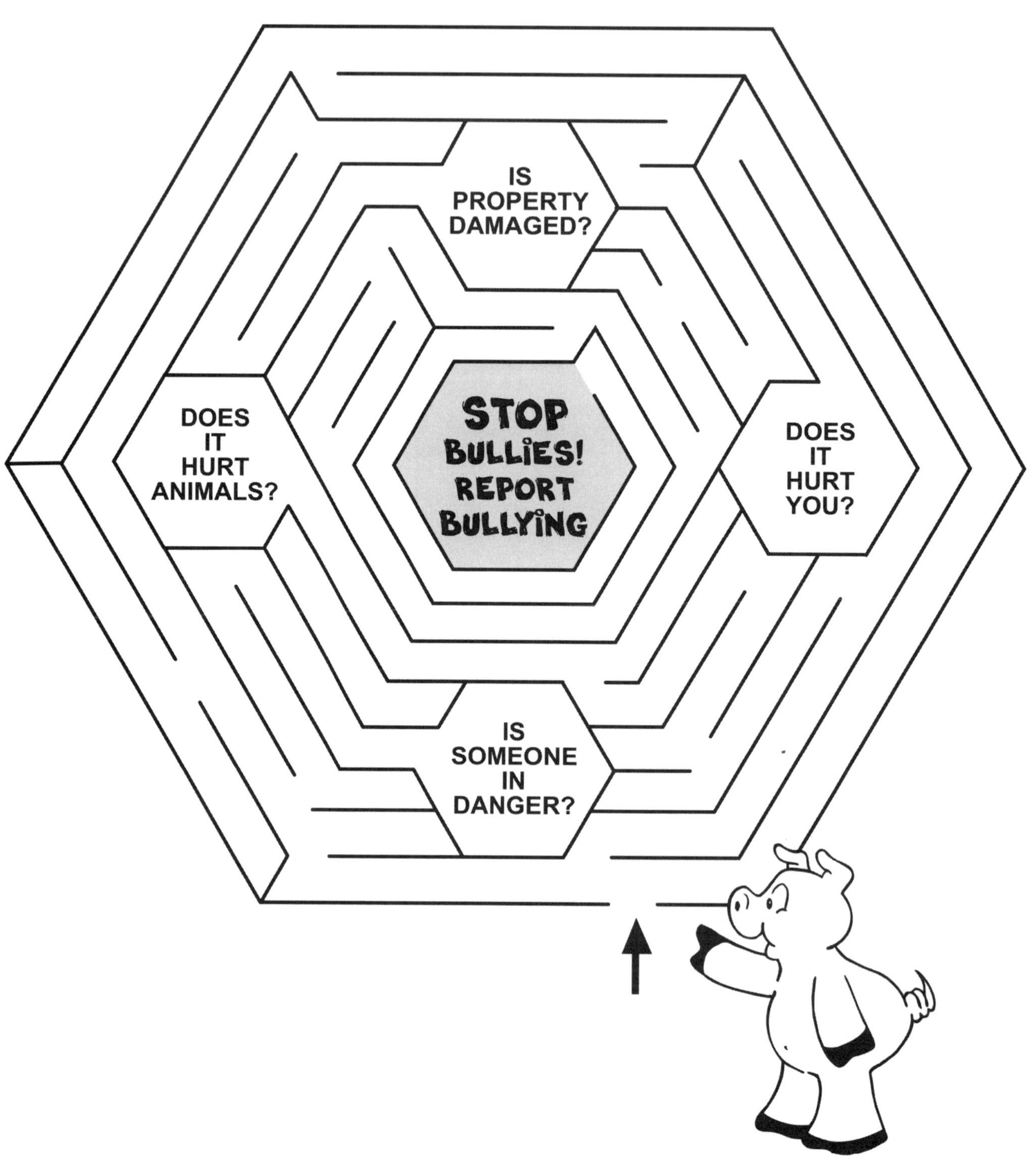

MEANNESS, TEASING, ROUGH STUFF

Purpose:

To help students understand that their words and actions can negatively affect others and that dismissing thoughtless words and actions as "just playing" does not excuse or lessen the damage harmful behavior does

Suggested Students:

Students referred because of problems with social skills, friendship, anger control, and/or aggressiveness

Grades K–3

Materials Needed:

For The Leader:
Rough Words/Soft Words Activity (K-3):
- ☐ *Rough Words/Soft Words Statements And Situations* reproduced on cardstock/heavyweight paper and cut apart (pages 73-74)
- ☐ Scissors
- ☐ Container

Optional Books:
- ☐ *Words Are Not For Hurting* by Elizabeth Verdick
- ☐ *Scrappy The Squabbler* by Ron Berry
- ☐ *The Band-Aid Chicken* by Becky Rangel Henton

For The Student:
Introduction:
- ☐ Drawing paper
- ☐ Crayons or markers

Rough Words/Soft Words Activity (K-3):
- ☐ Piece of sandpaper
- ☐ Fleece, velvet, or other soft material

Warm Fuzzy Art Activity (K-3):
- ☐ Pom-pom
- ☐ Wiggly eyes
- ☐ Glue
- ☐ Foam heart or heart cut from red construction paper

Rough/Soft Worksheet (K-3):
- ☐ Copy of *Rough/Soft Worksheet* (page 75)
- ☐ Pencil

Preparation:

Put the cut-apart *Rough Words/Soft Words Statements And Situations* into a container.

Introduction:

If you're including a storybook, begin by reading it to the student.

Give the student drawing paper and crayons or markers. Then continue the lesson by asking/saying:

> ***Has anyone ever told you that you were being mean?***
>
> ***Have you ever felt someone was being mean to you?***
>
> ***When we think about meanness, we usually think of a bully. Draw a picture of a bully for me.*** (The student will probably draw a large, scowling boy.)

Tell the student that his/her picture looks like what most people think of when they call someone a bully or say someone is mean. Then say:

> ***I've noticed that meanness can come from friends or classmates. Has that happened to you? Has a friend ever hugged you so tight it hurt? Or tickled you so long it became painful? Has a friend ever said anything to you that was rough or hurt your feelings?***
>
> ***Today, we're going to look at how we treat classmates and friends to see if our words or actions are rough or mean.***

Rough Words/Soft Words Activity (K–3):

Give the student a piece of sandpaper. Ask him/her to feel it and describe its texture. Then ask him/her to do the same with the soft material.

Have the student place the sandpaper and soft material on a table.

Tell the student you'll read words, sentences, or situation descriptions. After reading each one, hand the student the card. He/she must decide if what was read is rough or soft and place the paper on the sandpaper or the soft material.

Pulling one card from the container at a time, read the *Rough Words/Soft Words Statements And Situations.* After reading all the cards, go back to the cards where the student says he was just playing (Tyler & Jarvis) or joking (Pete & George). Ask:

> ***Does saying you were just playing or joking mean everything is OK?***
>
> ***Does it change anything?***
>
> ***Have you ever said this?***
>
> ***What response did you get?***
>
> ***Have you ever noticed that bullying behaviors are not about beating someone up, but rather doing mean things to classmates and friends?***
>
> ***Have you ever done any of these things or seen others do them?***

Emphasize that bullying, roughness, and meanness can be found in daily classroom routines if we do nothing about thoughtless words and actions.

Review some of the card statements, if necessary, to illustrate the point.

Warm Fuzzy Art Activity (K–3):

Ask if the student has ever heard of a *warm fuzzy.* Explain that this expression is sometimes used to describe the feeling a person has when someone does kind or thoughtful things.

Give the student a pom-pom, wiggly eyes, a heart, and glue.

Have the student assemble the warm fuzzy by gluing the pom-pom onto the heart, then gluing the eyes onto the pom-pom.

Tell the student to take the warm fuzzy home to remind him/her that using kind, soft words brightens the days of others.

Rough/Soft Activity Sheet (K–3):

Give the student a copy of the *Rough/Soft* activity sheet and a pencil. Tell him/her to cross out situations that are rough and circle illustrations that are soft.

Conclusion:

Summarize the lesson by saying: "You can attract more flies with honey than with vinegar."

Then ask:

> ***What do you think this expression means?***
>
> ***What things have you learned that match the expression?***
>
> ***In what situations this week could you have used honey (soft) instead of vinegar (rough)?***

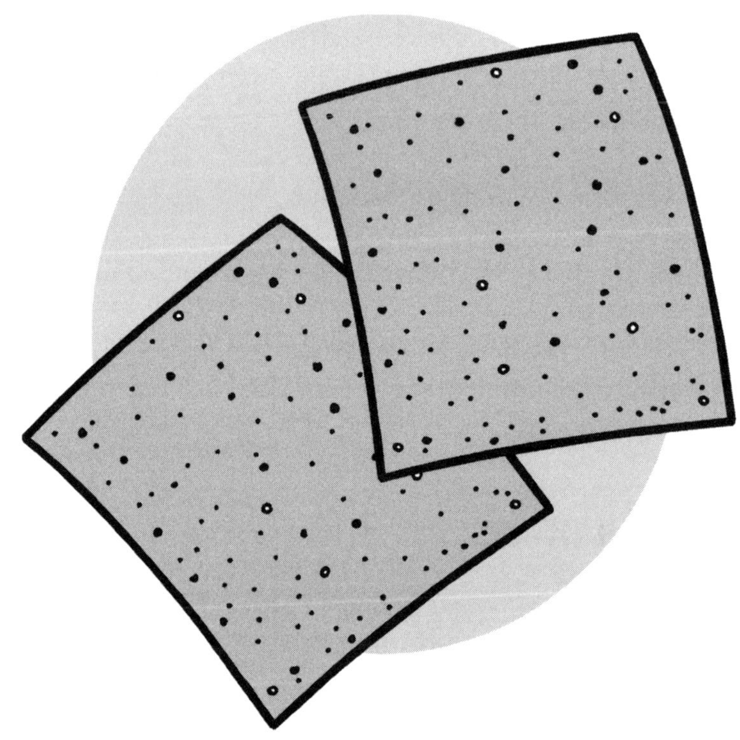

ROUGH WORDS/SOFT WORDS STATEMENTS AND SITUATIONS

Shut up!	Excuse me.
You act so stupid sometimes!	May I please get by?
I hate your guts.	You are really annoying.
Will you please sit down? I can't see around you.	I'm gonna stomp you!
What are you going to play at recess?	No offense, but I think you're fat.
You really get on my nerves.	How did you make that picture?

If Rosemary comes over, tell her our conversation is private and we want to be alone.	On the playground, a group of students pretends sticks are guns and "shoots" at other students.
A boy and a girl are hanging out at recess. When they return to the classroom, some students tease them by making kissing sounds and ask if they're going to get married.	Jackson falls and gets a bad scrape on his leg. John volunteers to get help.
Marissa comes late to class. Blake shows her what to do for the morning work.	Kiki gives Kelli a note. It says Kiki doesn't really like Taya and lists all the reasons Kelli should not like Taya.
DeMarcus notices Ashley's coat has fallen out of the cubby and is on the floor. DeMarcus hangs the coat in Ashley's cubby.	A group of boys is playing basketball at recess. When Braxton tries to join the game, the boys tell him he can't play because he stinks at basketball.
During seatwork, Pete and George get into an argument. George tells Pete he's going to punch him out. When Pete says he's going to tell, George says he was only joking.	During a pretend game of Power Warriors, Javaris jumps onto Tyler's back, forcing him to the ground. Tyler tells Javaris to get off, but Javaris says it's only a game and he's just playing.
Mia is cold in class. Polina lets Mia borrow her sweatshirt.	Maria starts to cry because she needs help figuring out what to write in her morning journal. The assignment is easy for Michael, who laughs and tells her she's acting like a baby.

ROUGH/SOFT WORKSHEET

Name ____

Directions: Cross out the students behaving roughly. Circle the students behaving softly.

A Note From Pamela Hudgins

I am an elementary school counselor with 20 years of experience in education. Married 20 years, I am the proud mother of three children, who are 10, 17, and 18 years old. As a family, we enjoy spending time on the Severn River. I'd like to thank my children for their inspiration, for often being guinea pigs when I'm trying out new ideas and lessons, and for their real-life knowledge and feedback about what it's like to be growing up in the 21st century.

I chose simple, hands-on activities that require little preparation time. The *Initial Interview* sheet helps me better understand my students. I conduct the interview when the child is calm, in a good mood, and willing to share personal thoughts. To begin building a strong working rapport, I also invite the child to ask me questions. The other activities actively involve the child in better understanding his/her emotions and how actions affect ourselves and others. A child who understands changing emotions is better able to take control and make positive decisions regarding family and peer relationships.

Pamela Hudgins is a counselor in Maryland and the author of *IChat Bingo*.

AIRPLANE RIDE

Purpose:

To help students learn to use visualizations and deep breathing to reduce tension, relax, and focus

Suggested Students:

Students who have been referred because of emotional outbursts and who need to learn self-control

Grades 2–8

Materials Needed:

For The Leader:
None

For The Student:
None

Activity:

The student sits comfortably with his/her head down. The student's eyes may be closed. Explain that during this activity, the student will learn to relax. Ask him/her to take a few deep breaths.

Read the following passage:

> ***You're at a busy airport. Notice all the people... the different sights... sounds... smells. You sit and wait to board your plane.***
>
> ***Your flight number is called. You're so excited! You board the plane, find your seat, and sit down. Notice how comfortable the seat is. You buckle up, sit back, and close your eyes. You hear the engines roar. The plane begins to move slowly. It picks up speed, then takes off.***
>
> ***You can't believe it! You've always wanted to visit this place. Your dream has come true. You'll be there in a few hours.***

Suddenly, you smell your favorite food. Breathe deeply. The flight attendant places the food on your tray. Eat the food. So good…

Then your favorite movie starts. What a lucky day!

You hear the captain announce that you'll be landing soon. Excitement grows…

The plane begins to descend. Landing…

You exit the plane. The views are just like the pictures. The smells are just as you imagined. You take a picture with your new camera so you'll always remember this day.

Raise your head.

Have the student describe the trip he/she just took. Then ask:

How do you feel?

When could you take a trip like this?

Have the student take a few moments to refocus and relax.

Conclusion:

Tell the student to remember the breathing and visualization he/she has just done, and to use these techniques whenever he/she has a sense of losing control.

BALL BOUNCE

Purpose:

To help the student hold a conversation with the counselor

Suggested Students:

Students referred because of having trouble sitting still and/or holding a conversation

Grades K–8

Materials Needed:

For The Leader:
- ☐ Soft playground ball

For The Student:
None

Activity:

Have the student stand approximately ten feet from you.

Explain that you're going to try to get a rhythm going by passing the ball back and forth, bouncing it between each pass.

Bounce the ball once, then toss it to the student.

Tell the student to catch the ball, then return it in the same manner.

When the student can do this without much concentration, bring up a topic that needs to be discussed.

The student will respond while playing catch. (*Note:* Students often talk more openly when engaged in physical activity.)

Conclusion:

When the conversation has ended, let the student know you appreciate his/her cooperation and ability to talk and play at the same time.

Follow-Up:

At your next meeting, remind the student how you passed the ball back and forth. Invite the student to suggest another way he/she can pass the ball to get a rhythm going. Rhythm is soothing and predictable. Students find it comforting and talk more openly and with less agitation than when they're asked to sit still.

INITIAL INTERVIEW

Purpose:

To develop the counselor/student relationship and help the counselor better understand the student

To help the student understand that someone cares and is interested in his/her life and feelings

Suggested Students:

Any referred students

Grades: K–12

Materials Needed:

For The Leader:

- ☐ Copy of *Interview Form* (pages 83-85)
- ☐ Pen or pencil

For The Student:

None

(*Note to the leader:* This interview helps break the ice and provides insight regarding the student and his/her feelings and support systems. It can help you decide how best to help the child succeed in school and with friends. These questions are meant to be conversation starters. Encourage the student to elaborate and let him/her know you're listening. The interview may be conducted at any point during the year and repeated months later as a follow-up. It's sometimes useful to jot notes in different colors on the original sheet to indicate any change.)

Activity:

Invite the student into your office. Explain that the purpose of the meeting is for you to develop an understanding of each other.

Tell the student that you're going to ask questions. Invite him/her to ask you questions.

Read the questions on the *Interview Form* and record the student's answers.

Conclusion:

Thank the student for cooperating. Evaluate the answers and record them on the comment portion of the *Interview Form.*

INTERVIEW FORM

Name: ______________________________

Date: ____________________ DOB ______________

Reason for referral: ______________________________

____

____

Self:

What do you like to do when you have free time? ______________

What do you do well? ______________________________

What would you like to do better? ______________________________

Tell me some of your favorites:

Favorite TV show ______________________________

Favorite movie ______________________________

Favorite sport ______________________________

Favorite activity ______________________________

Favorite book ______________________________

If you could be any animal, which would you most like to be? ______________

Why? ______________________________

If you could be any animal, which would you least like to be? ______________

Why? ______________________________

What's your typical day like? ______________________________

____

What's your favorite part of the day? ______________________________

____

Why? ______________________________

Name three wishes:

1. ______________________________
2. ______________________________
3. ______________________________

What makes you happy? ____________________

What makes you sad? ____________________

What confuses you? ____________________

What excites you? ____________________

What makes you angry? ____________________

For the older student, explore computer/chat room usage:

Do you read blogs or have a blog? ____________________

How much time a day do you spend on a computer? ____________________

Where is the computer? ____________________

Do you visit chat rooms? ____________________

Family:

Tell me about your family:

Where do you live? ____________________

What's your bedroom like? ____________________

What family member can you talk with when you're happy? ____________________

What family member can you talk with when you're sad? ____________________

What family member can you talk with when you're angry? ____________________

What family member can you talk with when you're confused? ____________________

Who understands you? ____________________

Do you have any pets? ____________________

What do you like about your family? ____________________

What would you like to change about your family? ____________________

Friends:

Tell me about your friends:

What do you like to do with them? ____________________

Who are your best friends? ____________________

Why? ____________________

Who is the biggest pain? ___

Why? ___

School:

Tell me about school:

What is your favorite subject? ___

What is your least favorite subject? ___

What do you like about school? ___

What would you like to change about school? ___

Additional Information:

Is there anything else you want me to know about you? ___

___

___

Is there anything else you want me to know about your family? ___

___

___

Is there anything else you want me to know about school? ___

___

___

___

Interpretation/Notes:

___

___

___

___

___

___

___

___

PUZZLE OF FEELINGS

Purpose:

To help the student understand the many different emotions he/she experiences

To help the student gain deeper self-awareness

To help the student understand how different situations evoke different feelings and responses

Suggested Students:

Students referred because they need help identifying and controlling their emotions

Grades K–8

Materials Needed:

For The Leader:
- ☐ Chart paper and marker

For The Student:
- ☐ 2 copies of the *Emotion Puzzle* (page 88)
- ☐ Pencil
- ☐ Scissors
- ☐ Envelope

(*Note to the leader:* This activity helps students understand that we all have many different feelings and emotions that are normal and OK if kept under control and expressed appropriately. This activity works best when the student is calm and ready to talk.)

Activity:

Session 1: Emotions

With the student, brainstorm different emotions. Record the emotions on chart paper.

Give the student the *Emotion Puzzle* and a pencil.

Have the student choose up to 16 emotions and write one on each piece of the puzzle. (*Note:* Younger children may want to draw faces showing emotions rather than write words on the puzzle pieces.)

Collect the *Emotion Puzzle.* Save it for the next session.

Session 2: How Do I Feel? What Do I Do?

With the student, review the *Emotion Puzzle* from the last session. Give the student another *Emotion Puzzle*. Tell him/her to pick four emotions, then write or draw each feeling word on a puzzle piece in the left column.

Discuss how the student typically behaves or feels when experiencing each of the four emotions he/she selected.

In the second column of puzzle pieces, have the student write or draw ideas as they relate to how he/she typically behaves or feels when experiencing each of the four emotions he/she selected.

Collect the *Emotion Puzzle*. Save it for the next session.

Session 3: Take Control

With the student, review the *Emotion Puzzle* from Session 2.

Tell the student to write or draw in the third column a socially acceptable way to act when experiencing the feelings in the first column. Help the student identify reactions and expressions that are appropriate when experiencing each emotion.

In the fourth column, help the student list ways to control his/her reactions.

Tell the student that he/she now has a visual/concrete representation of how he/she reacts when experiencing specific emotions and ways to take control.

Make a copy of the student's completed puzzle for your files. He/she may keep the original.

Give the student scissors and an envelope. Have him/her cut apart the 16 pieces of the puzzle, then reassemble it.

Engage the student in a conversation regarding the puzzle. Talk about ideas the student may have about his/her emotions and reactions.

Have the student put the puzzle pieces into the envelope. He/she may take the envelope home and keep the contents for review.

Conclusion:

Remind the student that he/she is in control and should not let emotions control him/her.

Follow-Up:

As a follow-up, the student can help you work with younger students, making puzzles and brainstorming appropriate reactions when experiencing emotions.

EMOTION PUZZLE

STICKS AND STONES

Purpose:

To help the student understand how our words and actions affect others

Suggested Students:

Students referred because of inappropriate social skills and lack of empathy

Grades 2–12

Materials Needed:

For The Leader:

- ☐ Clear bowl (9" works well, but any size will do)
- ☐ Several smooth stones, various sizes (usually available in a craft store or dollar store)
- ☐ Optional: Food coloring

For The Student:

None

Preparation:

Fill half the bowl with water. For a more dramatic effect, add a drop or two of food coloring.

Activity:

Discuss the cliché: "Sticks and stones may break my bones, but names will never hurt me" by asking:

> ***What does the saying mean?***
>
> ***What are your thoughts about name-calling?***
>
> ***How does name-calling affect others?***
>
> ***Does name-calling hurt others?***

Tell the student the bowl of water represents the school, community, peer group, or family.

Have the student choose several stones to represent hurtful words he/she might say.

Have the student drop one stone at a time into the bowl. As the student observes the effect the stones have on the water, point out how small ripples grow as they radiate from the middle of the bowl to the outside.

Discuss how this relates to name-calling, which starts out small, grows, and causes waves, just as the stones do in the water.

Describe the connection between smooth water, small waves, ripples, big storms, and how it takes a while for water to become smooth again after a storm.

Conclusion:

Ask:

> ***Now what do you think about "Sticks and stones may break my bones, but names will never hurt me"?***
>
> ***How do words hurt?***

Let the student keep one stone as a reminder that name-calling is hurtful.

A Note From Susan Jelleberg

I chose activities that I wrote and designed on an on-demand basis. The loss activity is based on the stages of grief identified by Elisabeth Kübler-Ross. Other activities, such as behavior modification, may be used by the counselor, teacher, or parents and/or monitored by the counselor. I wanted to suggest a variety of tools every counselor could use.

Susan Jelleberg lives in Bismarck, North Dakota. She is a North Dakota native whose educational experiences have occurred in North Dakota, South Dakota, and Minnesota. She holds a Bachelor of Science in art and psychology and a Master of Science in guidance and counseling. Besides working in public education, she has taught in four universities and colleges. Susan has also worked for the Girl Scouts of America and North Dakota Vocational Rehabilitation and has owned her own store.

The mother of Jenn, Frank, and Katie, Susan is the author of *Jellybean Jamboree* published by Mar*co Products.

FROM THE COUNSELOR'S DESK

General Referral For Individual And Group Goals For Parents And Teachers

The following form (pages 93-94) may be reproduced and distributed to classroom teachers, special needs teachers, and administrators. Although this valuable piece should be given out at the beginning of the school year, it may also be distributed at other times. Staff members should refer to this guideline when they believe a student needs counseling. Those ready to refer a student should check the appropriate items on the list or make an appointment to confer with the counselor.

The counselor should keep all referral forms in a student folder, which may also include IEPs and accounts of teacher-parent meetings, counselor-parent meetings, and the like. This referral form puts vital information at your fingertips for a staff or parent meeting.

FROM THE COUNSELOR'S DESK

General Referral For Individual And Group Goals For Parents And Teachers

Date ____________

Student's Name ________________________________

Staff Member's Name ______________________________

All individual or group counseling sessions are tailored to meet each student's goals. Student needs will determine how much we focus on various goals. Please check the things you feel would best meet this student's needs. If you prefer, visit with your counselor and discuss what you believe to be the student's needs.

FRIENDSHIP GOALS

Needs improvement in:

- ☐ Eye contact
- ☐ Social skills
- ☐ Friendship skills
- ☐ Self-esteem
- ☐ Following directions
- ☐ Coping skills
- ☐ Taking turns
- ☐ Cooperating
- ☐ Assertiveness vs. aggressiveness
- ☐ Self-concept
- ☐ Identifying and expressing feelings
- ☐ Organizational skills
- ☐ Verbal and non-verbal skills
- ☐ Listening skills
- ☐ Creativity
- ☐ Thinking skills and strategies
- ☐ Problem solving
- ☐ Empathy vs. sympathy
- ☐ Learning to utilize available resources

DIVORCE I GOALS

Needs improvement in:

- ☐ Understanding what divorce is and is not
- ☐ Understanding and using correct terminology
- ☐ Answering specific questions
- ☐ Defining feelings and expressing them appropriately
- ☐ Coping skills
- ☐ Listening skills
- ☐ Understanding that he/she isn't the only one whose parents have divorced
- ☐ Communication skills
- ☐ Learning to trust again
- ☐ Learning to visualize "gray" areas
- ☐ Developing and utilizing a support system
- ☐ Self-concept
- ☐ Self-esteem
- ☐ Thinking skills and strategies
- ☐ Empathy vs. sympathy
- ☐ Learning to utilize available resources

ANGER-CONTROL GOALS

Needs improvement in:

- ☐ Identifying "buttons" people push
- ☐ Identifying when and by whom buttons are pushed
- ☐ Developing coping strategies
- ☐ Understanding the meaning of *striking out*
- ☐ Identifying "rewards" of striking out
- ☐ Identifying "bad things" about striking out
- ☐ Identifying and utilizing alternatives to striking out
- ☐ Setting up goals and plans to change behavior
- ☐ Lessening competitive competition
- ☐ Developing and utilizing a support system
- ☐ Identifying physical symptoms before reaching the "breaking point"
- ☐ Utilizing self-talk
- ☐ Understanding and using "distancing"
- ☐ Learning to relax
- ☐ Identifying trigger thoughts and stresses and how to deal with them
- ☐ Identifying the three rules of anger

ASSERTIVENESS TRAINING

Needs improvement in:

- ☐ Defining and differentiating between *assertiveness* and *aggressiveness*
- ☐ Identifying role-play models
- ☐ Identifying and expressing feelings
- ☐ Recognizing her/his own rights and the rights of others
- ☐ Self-esteem
- ☐ Self-concept
- ☐ Reducing stage fright (talking in front of others)
- ☐ Designing and modeling appropriate assertiveness
- ☐ Responding appropriately to various scenarios
- ☐ Improving eye contact
- ☐ Recognizing present level of expressing anger and planning to improve communication

BLENDED FAMILIES
(must present Divorce I first)

Needs improvement in:

- ☐ Understanding what divorce is and is not
- ☐ Expanding *feeling words* vocabulary
- ☐ Expressing feelings
- ☐ Improving communication skills (including the Sandwich Technique)
- ☐ Gaining a support system, if not already in place
- ☐ Lessening feelings of isolation
- ☐ Acquiring better coping skills
- ☐ Enhancing problem-solving strategies
- ☐ Developing anger-control strategies
- ☐ Understanding the blended family and how to cope with different scenarios
- ☐ Strengthening the idea that he/she is still loved and now has more people to love

GRIEF THERAPY

Needs improvement in:

- ☐ Understanding the different stages of grief
- ☐ Understanding how different people express grief
- ☐ Identifying and expressing emotions
- ☐ Identifying acceptable and unacceptable ways to express grief
- ☐ Identifying anger's physical symptoms and ways to keep negative symptoms from escalating
- ☐ Communication skills
- ☐ Using relaxation techniques
- ☐ Alleviating guilt
- ☐ Developing empathy
- ☐ Alleviating isolation and loneliness

NOTES:

MAKING FRIENDS

Purpose:

To help the student identify situations and people that make him/her uncomfortable

To identify ways the student can verbally reach out to others

Suggested Students:

Students referred because of social or friendship concerns or shyness (See *General Referral For Individual And Group Goals* [pages 93-94] for desired outcomes of referral.)

Grades 3–8

Materials Needed:

For The Leader:
☐ Student's folder, if using one

For The Student:
☐ Copy of *Making Friends* (pages 97-98)
☐ Pen or pencil

Preparation:

Review the worksheet. Decide how many people you'd like the student to try talking with and in what capacity he/she should talk with them.

Activity:

With the student, review what you hope the counseling session will achieve (making new friends, alleviating shyness, becoming more comfortable around people, etc.).

Give the student a copy of *Making Friends* and a pencil. Have him/her complete the worksheet. (*Note:* If you feel that writing would make the student uncomfortable, read the questions aloud and record his/her answers.)

Review the completed worksheet and discuss the student's answers. Concentrate on the positive aspects of each question. When reviewing the three-step plan, ask what the student would do if things didn't go according to plan. Role-play the different scenarios the student suggests.

Have the student name his/her main friendship goal. If the goal is to make a new friend, write that and the name of the person the student wants to befriend on the back of the worksheet. If the goal is to learn to be friendly, write that goal on the worksheet.

Conclusion:

Before ending the session, make sure the student is prepared to try the plan. Tell him/her that at the next session, you'll talk about her/his successes.

If you're using a folder, place the worksheet in the student's folder.

MAKING FRIENDS

Student's Name ______________________ **Date** ____________

Who's most difficult for you to talk with? Adults? Girls? Boys? New people?

____

Name three times it's been difficult for you to talk with someone:

1. ____
2. ____
3. ____

What was going through your mind as you talked?

____

____

Why do you think it's difficult to talk with some people?

____

____

Who's easy for you to talk with? ______________________

Why? ____

____

List some things you've done to make it easier for you to talk with people:

____

____

____

Why do you think these ideas worked?

____

____

Many people go out of their way to avoid rejection. List some times you avoided being rejected.

____

____

____

What worries you most about talking with someone?

____

____

What's the worst thing that could happen if you talked with someone you were scared to talk with?

____

____

What's the best thing that could happen if you talked with someone you were scared to talk with?

____

____

Name some things you could talk about with:

Adults: _______________________________________

____

Boys: _______________________________________

____

Girls: _______________________________________

____

Write a three-step plan to talk with someone you are scared to talk with.

1. _______________________________________

2. _______________________________________

3. _______________________________________

During your next visit, talk with your counselor about what happened. Talk about the good things that happened, the things that didn't go so well, and how you felt before and after making the attempt. Decide if it was successful.

DIVORCE–FUN THINGS I DO WITH MY MOM AND DAD

Purpose:

To help the student see his/her parents as individuals with whom he/she can have different kinds of fun

Suggested Students:

Students referred because of a separation or divorce (See *General Referral For Individual And Group Goals* [pages 93-94] for desired outcomes of referral.)

Grades K–4

Materials Needed:

For The Leader:
- ☐ Chalkboard and chalk or chart paper and marker
- ☐ Student's folder, if using one

For The Student:
- ☐ Copy of *Fun Things I Do With My Mom* (page 101)
- ☐ Copy of *Fun Things I Do With My Dad* (page 102)
- ☐ Pencil
- ☐ Crayons or markers

Preparation:

Before you begin, note if the child hasn't seen or had contact with one or both parents for a long time. Your unawareness of this information could cause awkwardness for the child. You can later create a new lesson on missing a parent.

Activity:

Begin by asking:

> ***What do you do at recess?***
>
> ***Whom do you play with?***

Do you play with more than one friend?

Do you do the same things with each friend or do you like to do different things with different people?

Is it OK to like to do different things with different people? (Yes.) ***Why?*** (People have different likes and dislikes. If you have different friends, you have people with whom to do different things and you won't get bored.)

Introduce the idea of *brainstorming*. Explain that brainstorming is when you list all the ideas you can think of about a subject, then decide which ones are best.

Write *Mom* and *Dad* on the chart paper/chalkboard, making two columns. Ask the child to think about things he/she does with Mom. Write these on the chart paper/board under *Mom.*

Ask what things the child does with Dad. Write these under *Dad.*

Compare the two lists by asking:

What is the same?

What is different?

Why do you think the parent who lives with you does things differently than the parent who doesn't live with you? (Each parent has different interests, likes and dislikes, abilities, and financial resources. The parent who doesn't live with you usually wants the time you spend together to be fun.)

Give the student a copy of *Fun Things I Do With My Mom*, *Fun Things I Do With My Dad*, a pencil, and crayons or markers.

Have the child choose one worksheet and look at what is written on the chalkboard/chart paper in the column for that worksheet. Ask the child to choose from the list the thing that is the most fun and write or draw it on the worksheet. Then have the child select the second most-fun thing, and so on, until he/she has chosen five things. Repeat the activity with the other worksheet.

Reinforce the idea that people (even parents) are different by saying:

We can do different things with each parent, just like we do with our friends. This doesn't mean one parent is right and the other is wrong, and it doesn't change our love for them.

Conclusion:

Ask what the child learned today.

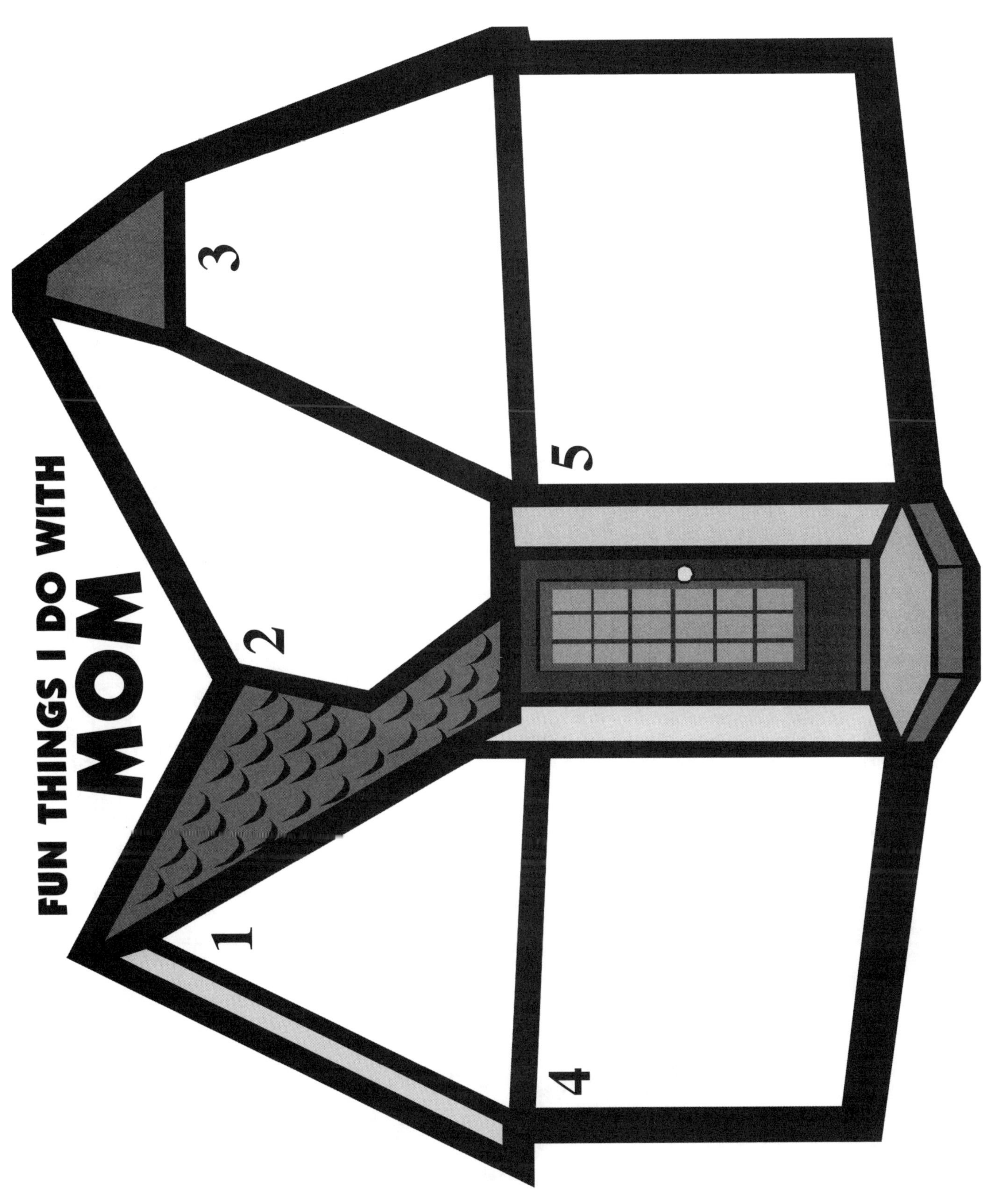
FUN THINGS I DO WITH
MOM
1
2
3
4
5

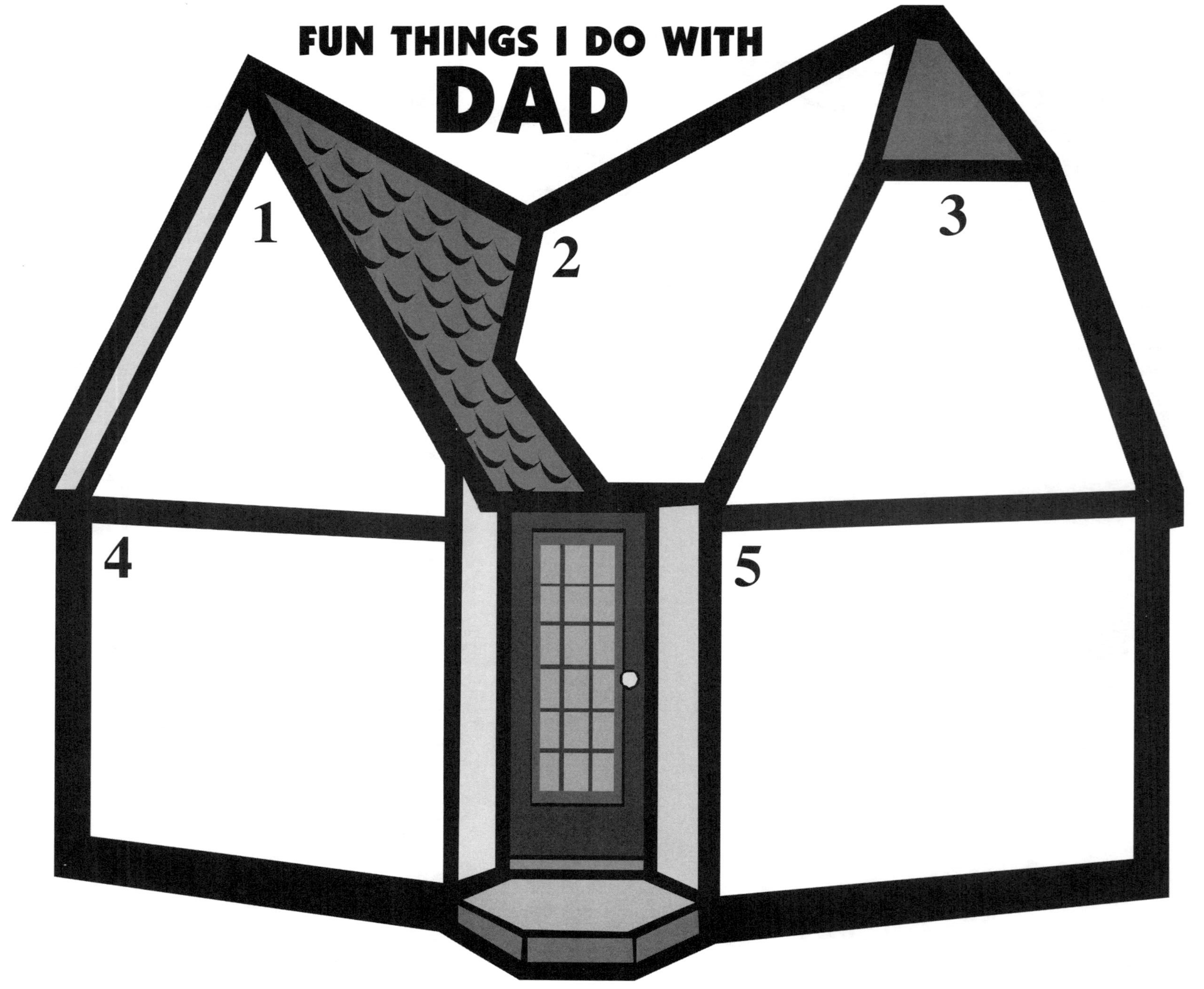
FUN THINGS I DO WITH
DAD
1
2
3
4
5

I NOSE I'M SPECIAL

Purpose:

To help the student identify what makes her/him special

Suggested Students:

Students referred because of low self-esteem or shyness (See *General Referral For Individual And Group Goals* [pages 93-94] for desired outcomes of referral.)

Grades K–3

Materials Needed:

For The Leader:
- ☐ Chalkboard and chalk or chart paper and marker
- ☐ Book with pictures of snowflakes (optional)
- ☐ Student's folder, if using one

For The Student:
- ☐ Copy of *I Nose I'm Special* (page 105)
- ☐ One 1 x 11" strip of paper
- ☐ Pencil
- ☐ Crayons or markers
- ☐ Glue stick

Activity:

Introduce the session by telling the student you'll be talking about what makes her/him special. Ask:

> ***What does the word* special *mean?*** (It means being not exactly the same as everyone else, being able to do things other people can't, having your own personality, etc.)

Explain that everyone is different. Even twins are not exactly the same. Say that it's kind of like snowflakes. (If you're using a book with pictures of snowflakes, show it at this time.)

Brainstorm with the student about how people can be special. Write these ideas on the chart paper/ chalkboard. You may wish to start by telling how you are special, then asking how the student is special.

Give the student a copy of *I Nose I'm Special,* the strip of paper, a pencil, crayons or markers, and a glue stick.

Explain that completing the paper will remind the student how special he/she is.

Ask the student what's missing on the *I Nose I'm Special* worksheet. Explain that he/she will be making the nose that's currently missing.

Ask the student to copy words that describe how special he/she is from the chart paper/chalkboard onto the back of the worksheet.

Show the child how to fold the paper accordion-style. Let him/her finish folding it.

Have the student put glue on the worksheet, then glue one end of the paper folded accordion-style to the worksheet to create a nose.

Let the student color the worksheet.

Conclusion:

Have the student explain what *special* means. Tell the child you believe he/she is special and to look at the *I Nose I'm Special* sheet to remember what is special about him/her.

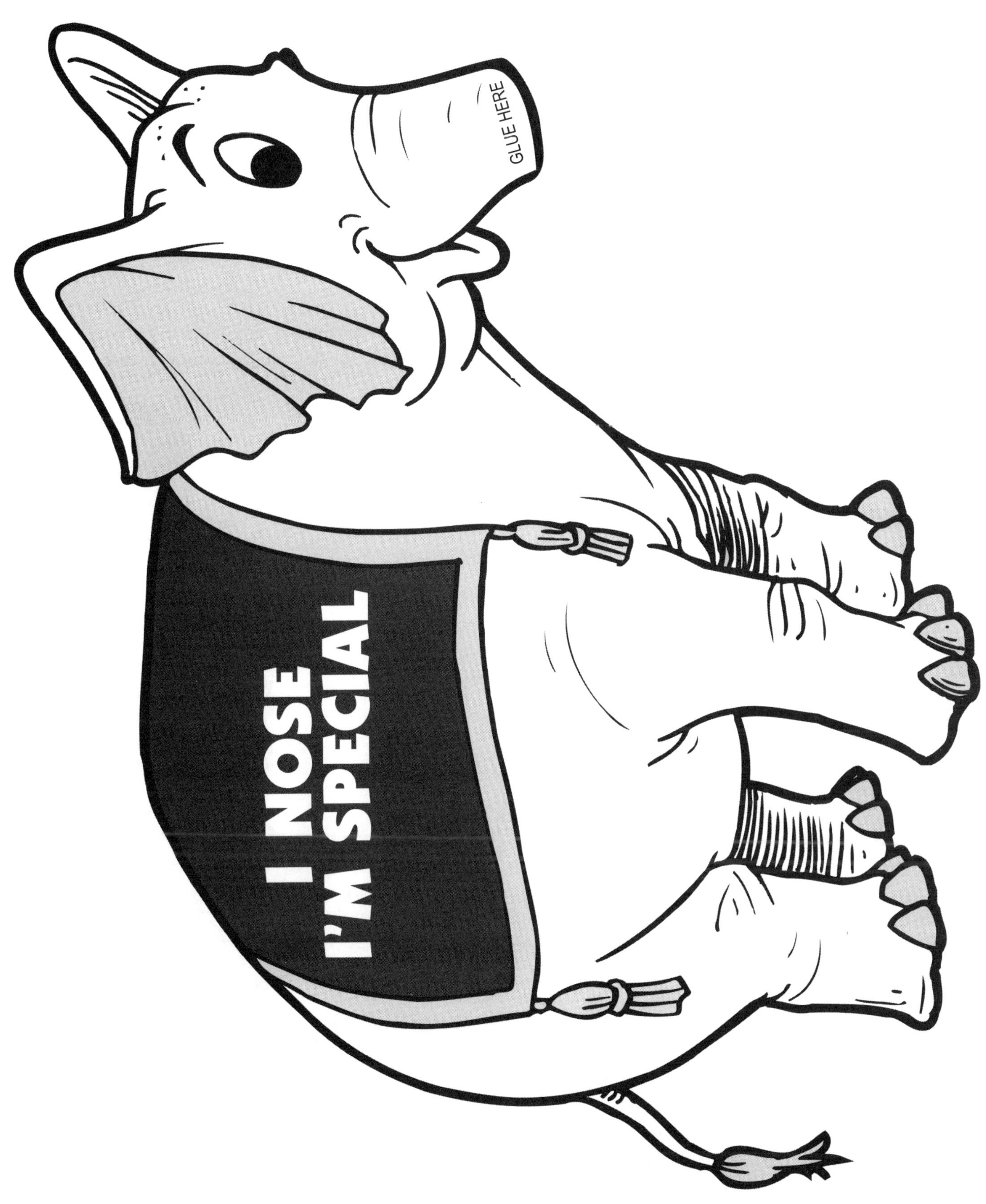
GLUE HERE
I NOSE
I'M SPECIAL

BEHAVIOR MODIFICATION WEEKLY TASK CHECK SHEETS

Purpose:

To keep track of the student's goals or chores

Suggested Students:

Students referred because of social concerns, work ethics, behavior problems, or goal-setting issues (See *General Referral For Individual And Group Goals* [pages 93-94] for desired outcomes of referral.)

Grades K–6

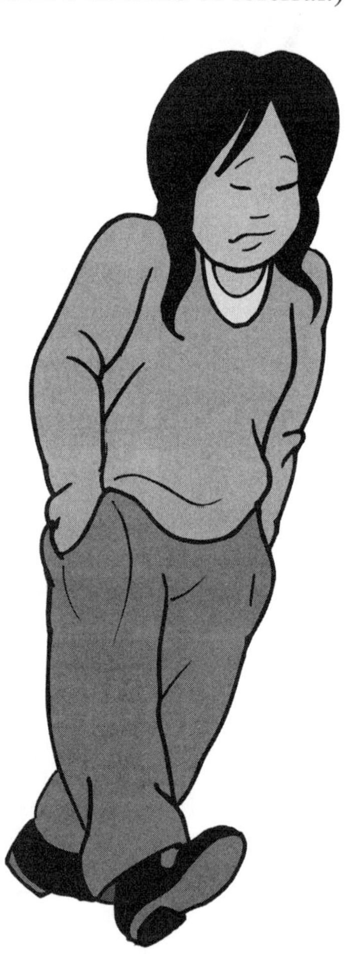

Materials Needed:

For The Leader:

- ☐ Stars or stickers

For The Older Student:

- ☐ 1 copy of the *Behavior Change Chart* per week (page 109)
- ☐ Pen or pencil
- ☐ Student folder, if using one

For The Younger Student:

- ☐ 1 copy of the *Behavior Change Chart* per week (page 109)
- ☐ Crayons or markers
- ☐ Magazines
- ☐ Glue or tape
- ☐ Scissors
- ☐ Student folder, if using one

Preparation:

Identify goals or chores that you, the parent(s)/guardian(s), or teachers wish to address with the student. (It's sometimes good to have the teacher(s) and parent(s)/guardian(s) present when reviewing this so everyone understands what is being done and questions can be answered.) Jointly decide on an appropriate initial number of goals or chores.

Most behavior-modification strategies are limited to three goals. For ADHD/ADD children or for a task-reminder checklist, you may use as many as the child can successfully handle. Don't overwhelm the child by beginning with too many goals or chores. You can always add more.

Some goals for home could be a get-ready-in-the-morning list, a completing-homework list, an evening or before-bed checklist, or a hygiene checklist.

Some goals for school could be attending school regularly, raising your hand when you want to speak, or not bothering classmates during work time.

Activity:

Tell the child which goals or chores the adults want to have addressed. Ask if the student feels she/he can work on these things.

Older child: Have the child write his/her selected goals or chores in the first column of the *Behavior Change Chart.*

Younger child: Help the child find and cut out magazine pictures and glue or tape them onto the *Behavior Change Chart.* You could also use crayons or markers to draw pictures of toothbrushes, beds, shampoo, hairbrushes, books, and other things to remind the child what his/her goals are.

Explain that a star or sticker will be placed in the slot for each day or time frame in which a task is completed. At the end of the week, the child will take the completed worksheet to the counselor, who may keep it in a folder or make a copy for his/her files and give the child a new worksheet for the upcoming week.

For children with short attention spans, divide each worksheet square into two or four smaller boxes. For example, if you want to record half-days, divide each square in half and label it AM and PM. Or divide each square into even shorter time periods. The student should receive rewards more than once a week.

If this is a chore/goal list for home, explain that the parent(s) will give the stars and rewards. The child may bring the completed worksheet to school to show the counselor. If this is a chore/goal list for school, the teacher may be in charge of recording the student's accomplishments and the counselor will hand out rewards.

Rewards should have little, if any, momentary value. Suggested rewards are:

- decide what to have for dinner
- spend extra time with one or both parents
- rent a movie
- stay up later on the weekend
- have a friend stay over

- spend extra time on the computer
- be read to by someone
- game time
- mall tokens
- being line leader
- art time

Conclusion:

End with words of encouragement to signify your faith in the student's ability to complete the assigned task.

NAME ______________________________

WEEK OF ___________________________

BEHAVIOR CHANGE CHART

Chore/Goal	SUN	MON	TUE	WED	THU	FRI	SAT

I CAN BE ANYTHING I WANT!

Purpose:

To demonstrate that even though there are some things the student can't do well, he/she can do other things very well

Suggested Students:

Students referred because of low self-esteem, anger, regression, or friendship issues (See *General Referral For Individual And Group Goals* [pages 93-94] for desired outcomes of referral.)

Grades 3–6

Materials Needed:

For The Leader:
- ☐ Pictures and/or names from the list of *Famous People With Disabilities* (pages 112-113)
- ☐ Student's folder, if using one

For The Student:
- ☐ Copy of *I Can Be Anything I Want!* (page 114)
- ☐ Pencil or crayons or markers

Activity:

Ask the student:

> ***Do you know why you're visiting with me today?***
>
> ***Are there things that make you feel bad?***

Have the child talk about feeling bad as a result of not being able to do things well.

Explain that lots of famous people who did poorly in grade school did well in life. Ask:

> ***Do you know who the creator of* Mickey Mouse *and* Donald Duck *was?*** (Walt Disney)
> ***Walt Disney was fired from his first job because "he didn't have any good ideas."***

Have you ever heard of Air Jordan? (Michael Jordan) ***He didn't make the basketball team the first time around in high school.***

How about Thomas Edison, the inventor? He tried 2,000 times before he made a light bulb.

Use the *Famous People With Disabilities* list and/or pictures of famous people to illustrate that people who can't do everything well can do some things well. The things we do well are called *strengths,* and the things we can't do as well are called *limitations.* Ask the child to define *limitations.*

Tell the child to try her/his best even when it seems no one seems to believe in her/him. Say:

Look at all the names on the **Famous People With Disabilities** ***list. They believed in themselves. Look what they accomplished!***

On the *I Can Be Anything I Want* worksheet, have the student write or draw things he/she can do well and name things he/she could improve upon with practice.

Conclusion:

Remind the child that if we work on doing something well, we can improve our skills. But if we never try, we'll never get better at it.

Let the child take home some pictures or have her/him write the names of the famous people on the back of the worksheet.

FAMOUS PEOPLE WITH DISABILITIES

NAME OF PERSON	OCCUPATION	TYPE OF DISABILITY
Tiger Woods	Professional Golfer	Stuttering
Albert Einstein	Inventor/Scientist	Dyslexia
Alexander Graham Bell	Inventor Of Telephone	LD
Ludwig Beethoven	Composer	Deafness
Bill Clinton	US President	Hearing Disability
Christopher Reeves	Actor, Director, Activist	Quadriplegia
Dwight D. Eisenhower	US President	Stuttering
Emily Dickinson	Poet	Agoraphobia
Franklin Delano Roosevelt	US President	Polio (inability to walk unassisted)
Harriet Tubman	Rescuer Of Slaves	Epilepsy, Narcolepsy (inability to stay awake)
Helen Keller	Activist for rights of blind and visually impaired	Blindness, Deafness, Muteness* (*during early childhood)
Jackie Stewart	Race Car Driver	LD

Jim Abbot	Athlete	Born With Only One Hand
Julius Caesar	Politician And Leader	Epilepsy
Leonardo da Vinci	Artist, Sculptor, Painter	Epilepsy
Louis Braille	Invented Braille System For Reading By Touch	Blindness
Lucille Ball	Comedian, Actor	Childhood Rheumatoid Arthritis
Marilyn Monroe	Actor And Singer	Stuttering, Depression
Princess Diana	Humanitarian	Eating Disorders
Rodney Dangerfield	Comedian, Actor	Depression
Ronald Reagan	US President And Former Actor	Hearing Disability
Sylvester Stallone	Actor	LD
Theodore Roosevelt	US President	Asthma, Poor Vision
Thomas Edison	Inventor	Hearing Problem
Wolfgang Amadeus Mozart	Composer	Tourette Syndrome
Wright Brothers	Invented The Airplane	LD

I CAN BE ANYTHING I WANT

SOME BUNNY

Purpose:

To help the student understand that it's important to love yourself

Suggested Students:

Students referred because of social concerns, shyness, lack of confidence, or friendship issues (See *General Referral For Individual And Group Goals* [pages 93-94] for desired outcomes of referral.)

Grades K–4

Materials Needed:

For The Leader:
- ☐ Optional: Storybook about love
- ☐ Student's folder, if using one

For Each Student:
- ☐ Copy of *Some Bunny Loves You* (page 117)
- ☐ Cotton ball
- ☐ Crayons or markers
- ☐ Glue

Activity:

If you're using a storybook about love, begin by reading and discussing the book.

Then continue the lesson by asking:

> ***Have you ever held a bunny or a kitten?***
>
> ***How did you feel?***
>
> ***Do you have any pets or special toys that you love?***

Explain that there are different kinds of love. Loving a teddy bear isn't the same as loving a parent. Loving ice cream is different from loving a pet.

Then ask:

How do you know someone loves you? (You feel it or he/she tells you.)

How do you know when an animal loves you?

How do you know when you love something?

Ask the following questions. Discuss the answers.

Who is the most important person to love you? (The most important person is the student him/herself.) ***Why?*** (Because when you love yourself, it's easier to love other people. When you don't like yourself, it's hard to like other people.)

Do you like yourself better at some times than at others?

What are the times you don't like yourself very well?

Then say:

When you don't like yourself very well, remember that there are lots of good things to like about yourself. When you feel that way, it can help to talk with or be around people who support you.

Give the student a copy of *Some Bunny Loves You*, crayons or markers, a cotton ball, and glue. Explain that he/she may keep the worksheet as a reminder to love him/herself. (*Note:* The student may give the worksheet to someone to remind that person that he/she is loved.)

Have the student put her/his name on the activity sheet and complete the sheet. Give the following instructions:

Stretch the cotton ball slightly to fit the tail area, Don't stretch the cotton ball too much or it will get holes in it.

Once the cotton ball is stretched, glue it onto the tail area on your worksheet. Use only a drop or two of glue. If you use too much glue, the worksheet will be hard to color.

Ask if the student has any questions. If not, let him/her begin the activity. Don't let the student use too much glue.

After the cotton ball tail is glued on, tell the student to color the worksheet.

Conclusion:

End by reviewing what *love* means and why it's important to love ourselves.

Some Bunny
Loves You
MY NAME

A Note From Arden Martenz

Art therapy is one of the techniques I've relied on most when working with students. I often found an elementary student had not the slightest idea why he/she was seated in my office. Many of these students were reluctant to talk because they weren't sure what to talk about. They loved playing games, but an art activity was a more effective way to establish rapport and gain insight. Because young children draw freely and enthusiastically, art has always been an integral part of my individual counseling.

I've also found sentence-completion activities to be beneficial. Because students of different ages and in different situations need different sentence-completion activities, I always kept a variety at my fingertips. Doing the writing enabled me to move the activity along and complete it in the allotted time. I found that most of my students really didn't want to write. They'd been writing in class, and looked at this as another assignment. This was not my objective. I also found that a student who came to a sentence that was difficult to complete would waste valuable time pondering what to put down. And I found students to be more open when speaking than when writing. It seemed that when they had to put things on paper, they became apprehensive.

Arden Martenz, a former Pennsylvania counselor, is president of Mar*co Products. She is the author and co-author of more than 30 books, including *Awesome Activities, Groups To Go Grades 3–5,* and *Groups To Go Grades K–3.* In 2000, she was named one of the outstanding educators of the 20th century for Bucks County, Pennsylvania.

INITIAL INTERVIEW TECHNIQUE

Purpose:

To help the counselor understand what the student thinks of him/herself

Suggested Students:

Students referred because of low self-esteem or inappropriate behaviors

Grades K–8

Materials Needed:

For The Leader:

- ☐ 18 x 24" construction paper (white and various colors)
- ☐ Crayons or markers
- ☐ Table

For The Student:

None

Activity:

Place the art materials on a table. Have the student select markers/crayons and one piece of paper. (*Note:* Colored paper makes it easier for some students to begin, as they feel they've been given a starting point.)

Ask:

> ***Will you write your name on the paper?*** (The words "will you write" tell the child that he/she is not *expected* to write. A child who can't write will be discouraged by hearing that he/she should be able to write. So that wording should be avoided.)
>
> ***What kind of girl/boy are you?*** (If the student isn't sure what you mean, provide clues such as "Are you happy?" You may need to write the words on the paper for younger students. Older students can write the words themselves. If you've written the words, read them aloud to make sure what you've written is what the student means.)

Have the student draw a symbol, such as the sun or a tree, that is most like him/her or draw the animal he/she would most like to be. (*Note:* For additional insight into the drawing, ask the student to explain the reason for his/her selection.)

Collect the drawing.

Conclusion:

After the student leaves, make notes on a separate paper about what the drawing and student's reasons for the selection reveal about his/her self-image.

PERSONAL PORTFOLIO

Purpose:

To show the student his/her strengths

Suggested Students:

Students referred because of low self-esteem

Grades K–8

Materials Needed:

For The Leader:
- ☐ Paper
- ☐ Pencil
- ☐ Various colors of 18 x 24” construction paper
- ☐ Stapler and staples

For The Student:
- ☐ White drawing paper
- ☐ Crayons or markers

Activity:

This activity spans a period of time. The counselor may choose to make the student’s personal portfolio any length.

Ask:

> ***What kind of things do you like to do?*** (Sports, video games, school subjects, etc. Note the student’s responses.)

Based on the student’s answers, decide how many topics to include in the portfolio. Be sure to select those you feel are meaningful to the student.

Select a topic at each meeting. Give the student drawing paper and crayons or markers. Have the student draw positive things about him/herself in relation to the topic, realizing that there may be more than one drawing per topic. If the topic is sports, for example, the student may want to draw more than one sport. A student who does several things well in a particular sport may want to draw each activity.

Conclusion:

End by discussing the strengths the student has drawn and how valuable they are in relation to the topic. If the child has drawn one or more things about baseball, for example, discuss how the student's actions are important to the team.

Collect the student's work and save it for the final session.

At the final session, have the student select a piece of colored construction paper. Staple the pictures into a booklet and have the student draw a cover on the colored paper. The completed portfolio will contain an illustrated story of the student's strengths.

FAMILY PORTRAIT

Purpose:

To demonstrate how the student sees him/herself in relation to the family situation and how that perception reflects the student's self-concept

Suggested Students:

Students referred because of low self-esteem, academic problems, behavior problems, and issues involving interpersonal relationships

Grades K–8

Materials Needed:

For The Leader:
None

For The Student:
- ☐ White drawing paper
- ☐ Crayons or markers

Activity: (This activity may be presented in several ways.)

Technique #1: Family Portrait (People)

Give the student drawing paper and crayons or markers.

Ask the student to draw a picture of his/her family.

As the student is completing his/her drawing, note the position of the family members, the order in which they're drawn, and any outstanding features of the drawing. The position of each family member can tell you how the student sees groups within the family structure. For example, a student experiencing divorce may draw a picture of his/her mother and father holding hands. This tells the counselor that the drawing represents the student's wish, rather than reality. The student who draws everyone except him/herself can reveal feelings of unimportance. The first family member the student draws is usually the person he/she feels is most important. Other things to look for are:

- the only person who isn't smiling.
- one family member who is much larger than the others, indicating dominance.
- a missing family member, whose absence may indicate insignificance.
- a family divided into two parts, with some members closer to the father and some closer to the mother.
- everyone close together, holding hands.
- an absent mother or father portrayed by a picture on the wall.
- some family members apart from others.

When the student's drawing is completed, number the figures in the sequence in which they were drawn. Have the student confirm or deny any thoughts you may have formed while he/she was drawing.

Technique #2: Family Portrait (Homes)

Have the student draw his/her home. The house should be open, like the back of a doll's house. Allow the student to furnish the rooms or leave them empty.

The student should then draw his/her family, placing each family member in the room in which that person spends the most time, doing what he/she most often does in that room. (*Note:* This picture can reveal if everyone is involved in family life, who is productive, etc.)

Technique #3: Family Portrait (Family Zoo)

This exercise is similar to having a student draw an animal he/she would like to be. In this exercise, the student not only shows what animal he/she would like to be, but how he/she perceives each family member.

Have the student draw each family member as a zoo animal, farm animal, or sea creature.

Look for family members who are:

- powerful animals like lions and elephants.
- playful or mischievous animals like monkeys.
- quiet animals like giraffes.
- friendly animals like deer. (Deer are really *not* friendly, but the child may have been influenced by animated cartoons.)

Discuss why the student chose each animal.

Conclusion:

After the student leaves, make notes on a separate piece of paper about what the drawing selections and the reasons given for them reveal about the student's self-image.

COOPERATIVE DRAWING

Purpose:

To have the student complete a cooperative drawing with the counselor

Suggested Students:

Students who need encouragement to draw and those whose inability to share is causing difficulty in peer relationships

Grades K–8

Materials Needed:

For The Leader:

None

For The Student:

- ☐ White drawing paper
- ☐ Crayons or markers

Activity:

Give the student drawing paper and crayons or markers. Say that the two of you are going to draw a picture together, one line at a time.

Have the student select the topic. (*Note*: An alternate idea is to not have any topic and see where the drawing takes you.)

Explain that the student will start by drawing one line. If the drawing is of a sailboat on the ocean, for example, the student may choose to draw one line across the page to represent the ocean or may start to draw the boat. The counselor will then add to the picture by drawing another line for the boat or, perhaps, draw waves on the ocean. Each person draws one line that is a continuation of the line the other person has just drawn. When the lines can no longer be continuous, the person's turn is over and the next person begins.

Conclusion:

End by talking about how the picture looks and why the student chose that topic. (If the student didn't choose a topic, discuss how the picture was created when you hadn't decided what to draw.)

Then ask:

> ***Would you rather have drawn the picture by yourself?***
>
> ***Would you like to draw a picture like this with another student?***
>
> ***What did you like best about drawing a picture this way?***
>
> ***What did you like least about drawing a picture this way?***

The student's answers and response to the drawing allow the counselor to determine the best course of action to take in future sessions.

THREE WISHES

Purpose:

To help the counselor understand the student's value system

Suggested Students:

Students referred because of low self-esteem, academic problems, behavior problems, and issues involving interpersonal relationships

Grades K–8

Materials Needed:

For The Leader:

None

For The Student:

☐ White drawing paper
☐ Crayons or markers

Activity:

Give the student drawing paper and crayons or markers.

Tell the student he/she may have three wishes. Explain that although the wishes cannot be granted, the student should pretend that the exercise is real and that his/her wishes will be granted.

Have the student draw the three wishes.

Conclusion:

Discuss why the student chose these wishes.

Based on the drawing and the student's response, determine if the wishes indicate materialistic desires, concerns for other people, self-centeredness, or any other character trait.

SENTENCE COMPLETION

Purpose:

To obtain insights into a student's beliefs

Suggested Students:

Students referred for any reason have responded well to this activity

Grades K–8

Materials Needed:

For The Leader:

- ☐ Copy of chosen *Sentence Completion* (pages 130-135)
- ☐ Pen

For The Student:

None

Preparation:

Reproduce the *Sentence Completion* activity that best meets the student's needs.

Activity:

Introduce the activity by telling the student that you'll read aloud the beginnings of some sentences. The student should complete each sentence with the first word or words that come to mind. Explain that you will record the student's answers.

Read each sentence on the selected *Sentence Completion* worksheet. Record the answers as quickly as possible, moving from one sentence to the next without comment. Highlight any responses that strike you as important.

Conclusion:

After the student leaves, review his/her answers. Note how the highlighted responses may indicate the student's primary personality traits, values, and other outstanding characteristics.

SENTENCE COMPLETION #1
(For Use With Academic Referrals)

Name ______________________________ **Grade** ____________

Class ______________________________ **Date** ____________

1. Something I'd like to learn to do is ______________________________.
2. One person I've learned a lot from is ______________________________.
3. I'm glad I've learned to ______________________________.
4. One important thing I'm learning in school is ______________________________.
5. Something I've learned from my friends is ______________________________.
6. One thing I could teach someone else is ______________________________.
7. One thing I didn't know before I came to school is ______________________________.
8. I wish everyone would learn ______________________________.

SENTENCE COMPLETION #2

(For Use With Academic Referrals)

Name ______________________________ **Grade** ____________

Class ______________________________ **Date** ____________

1. School is ______________________________.
2. I have trouble learning when ______________________________.
3. I wish my teacher would ______________________________.
4. Homework is ______________________________.
5. One thing I'm glad I learned this year is ______________________________.
6. Math is ______________________________.
7. I get into trouble when ______________________________.
8. Science is ______________________________.
9. One book I liked to read was ______________________________.
10. One book I did not like to read was ______________________________.
11. One good thing about my class is ______________________________.
12. Social studies is ______________________________.
13. My best subject is ______________________________.
14. I could get better grades if ______________________________.
15. One thing I would change about school is ______________________________.

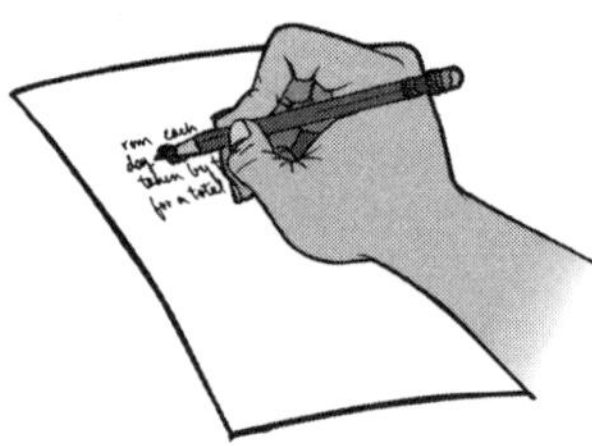

SENTENCE COMPLETION #3

(For Use With Children With Self-Esteem Issues)

Name ________________________ **Grade** __________

Class ________________________ **Date** __________

1. I can never ______________________________.
2. Someday, I ______________________________.
3. When I look in the mirror, I ______________________________.
4. One thing that makes me mad is ______________________________.
5. I'm happy when ______________________________.
6. I'm sad when ______________________________.
7. I'd like to be like ______________________________.
8. I wish my friends would ______________________________.
9. When I'm alone, ______________________________.
10. I'm best at ______________________________.

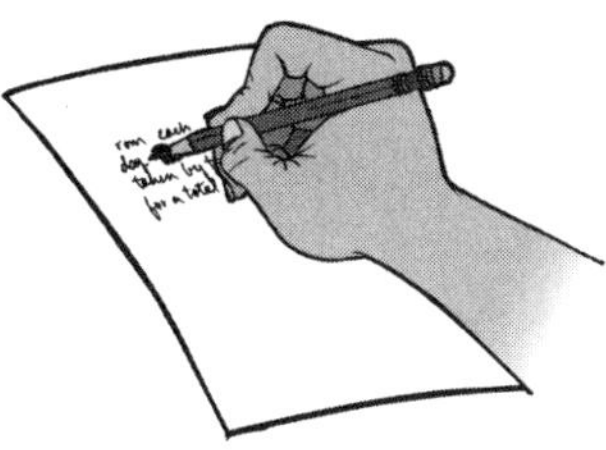

SENTENCE COMPLETION #4

(For Use With Interpersonal Relationship Referrals)

Name ______________________________ **Grade** __________

Class ______________________________ **Date** __________

1. I wish ______________________________.
2. A friend should ______________________________.
3. It's important to ______________________________.
4. I feel bad when ______________________________.
5. Other kids ______________________________.
6. Tattling makes ______________________________.
7. I can't understand why ______________________________.
8. I don't like ______________________________.
9. If I could have only one friend, he/she would be ______________________________.
10. One thing I would do for a friend is ______________________________.
11. One thing I would not do for a friend is ______________________________.
12. Friends ______________________________.
13. If my friend was sad, I would ______________________________.
14. I feel left out when ______________________________.
15. I wish ______________________________.

SENTENCE COMPLETION #5

(For Use With Academic Referrals)

Name ______________________ **Grade** __________

Class ______________________ **Date** __________

1. School is ______________________.
2. My favorite subject is ______________________.
3. Teachers should ______________________.
4. Homework is ______________________.
5. My favorite time of day is ______________________.
6. One thing I like about math is ______________________.
7. My least favorite subject is ______________________.
8. If I were principal, I would ______________________.
9. My friends think I'm good at ______________________.
10. Tests make me ______________________.
11. One thing teachers don't do is ______________________.
12. One thing I don't like about reading is ______________________.
13. My favorite grade in school was/is ______________________.
14. One thing I'd like to learn more about in science is ______________________.
15. Every morning, ______________________.
16. One thing I don't like about math is ______________________.
17. One thing I'd like to learn more about in social studies is ______________________.
18. I wish I could spell ______________________.
19. My grades ______________________.
20. My parents worry ______________________.

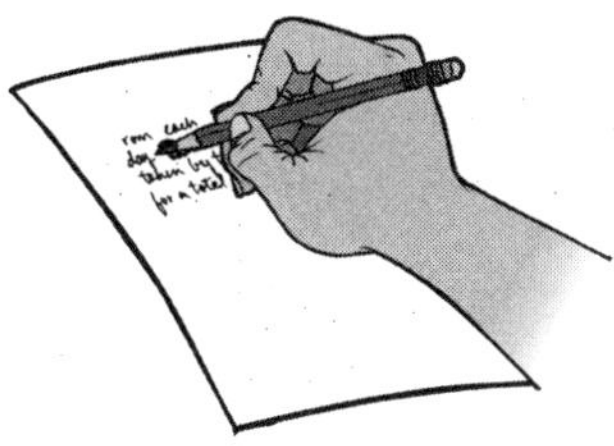

SENTENCE COMPLETION #6
(For Use With Behavior Referrals)

Name ______________________________ **Grade** ____________

Class ______________________________ **Date** ____________

1. Good behavior is when ______________________________.
2. Teachers don't like ______________________________.
3. Kids who hit other kids ______________________________.
4. The worst trouble I was ever in was ______________________________.
5. When kids pick on you, ______________________________.
6. Mothers don't like ______________________________.
7. When I get mad, I ______________________________.
8. My best friend is ______________________________.
9. I like my best friend because ______________________________.
10. Dads don't like ______________________________.
11. One thing that really makes me mad is ______________________________.
12. I could do better in school if ______________________________.
13. Other kids don't like ______________________________.
14. A bully is someone who ______________________________.
15. Things would be better in school if ______________________________.

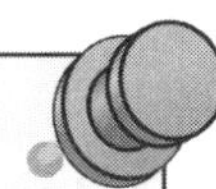

A Note From Melissa Richards

I utilize practical, goal-oriented strategies to help children in the therapeutic process, and I chose to address counseling topics that reflect typical issues students face. I believe it's vital to establish a safe and inviting environment in which the child feels comfortable working through difficult issues. I utilize open-ended questions to gain an understanding of the problem, then focus the session on goals. There's very little time in a school setting to spend on individual counseling, so it's important to address issues directly and deal with distractions that hinder the learning process. Because I believe it's necessary to maintain a solid level of trust between student and counselor, I always ask the student's permission before discussing the session with others. Parents/guardians and teachers can provide tremendous support, and I like to include them when appropriate.

Melissa Richards has a bachelor's degree in psychology and a master's degree in school counseling. An elementary school counselor for 12 years with the Albany-Flloyd County School Corporation in southern Indiana, she has taught as an adjunct professor in the counseling department at Indiana University Southeast and served as mentor for many practicum and internship students. She believes that being a school counselor is the most rewarding occupation possible. Solving problems, teaching, comforting, supporting, assisting, caring, sharing, and mentoring make her school days feel short, but quite worthwhile.

She is the author of *I Didn't Know I Was A Bully* and *I Didn't Know I Could Be The Child Left Behind.*

SEPARATION ANXIETY

Purpose:

To help the student work through separation anxiety at school

Suggested Students:

Students who have difficulty separating from their parent(s)/guardian(s) in order to attend school

Grades K–1

Materials Needed:

For The Leader:
- ☐ Office area separate from the classroom
- ☐ Schedule of class events for the day (special classes/activities)

For The Student:
- ☐ Objects/Activities for play therapy (Coloring supplies, sand, modeling clay, building blocks)

Preparation:

Students are usually referred by a phone call or visit from a parent/guardian to report the child crying and not wanting to attend school. Ask questions to get an understanding of any circumstances that could distress the child. Encourage a parent/guardian to acknowledge the child's feelings, then tell the child that he/she must go to school. Advise the parent/guardian to try to redirect the conversation to another subject. If other issues are causing distress, counsel the child or make an appropriate referral.

Ask the parent/guardian what his/her typical day will be like while the child is at school. Tell the child how busy his/her parent/guardian is and how he/she needs the child to attend school.

If a teacher refers the student to you, attempt to contact the parent/guardian to ask what could be distressing the child.

Encourage a child who's clinging to the parent/guardian to come to your office for a few minutes. Ask him/her to say "goodbye" to the adult left behind. If necessary, take the child to your office and tell the adult you'll report later in the day. The child will probably calm down within minutes of leaving the parent/guardian.

Activity:

When the student is in the counselor's office and calm enough to talk, ask about his/her feelings. (*Note:* If the child is non-verbal, offer him/her something to do such as sand play, modeling clay, coloring, building blocks, etc.)

Address the issue of separation anxiety by saying:

Tell me why you're crying and why you don't want to come to school.

Discuss the student's responses. If his/her reason is school-related, explain that you can help with those problems. If the reason is that the child will miss his/her parent/guardian, talk about how busy that person will be while the child is in school.

Talk about all the tasks and activities the teacher has planned for the child's day. Ask the child about friends in the classroom. Tell the child how those friends miss him/her.

Once the child is calm, take him/her to class. Say:

I'll be checking on you several times today.

Tell the teacher you'll be checking on the student. When you check on him/her, do it quietly or just make eye contact.

Your purpose is to present yourself BRIEFLY as someone the student can trust and to whom he/she can transfer feelings of dependence. When you call, reassure the parent/guardian that the child is fine. Explain that you'll greet the child when he/she arrives at school. Encourage the parent/guardian not to enter the building, as this only prolongs and increases the distress of separation.

At your final check that day, tell the child you'll meet him/her at the bus or car the next morning. This lets the child know to expect you.

The Next Morning:

Meet the child's bus or car. If the child is crying, take him/her to your office and talk briefly about his/her feelings, activities for the day, and classroom friends. Talk about the parent/guardian's busy day and the need for the child to be at school. Play while talking, if necessary, to distract the child from crying.

As soon as the child is calm, take him/her to class. Tell the child you'll check on him/her throughout the day.

Following Days:

This pattern is repeated, but the child should need to spend less time with the counselor each day. Gradually decrease the number of times you meet the child in the morning and how often you check on him/her during the day. Praise the child's independence. This process typically takes only a few days.

(*Note:* The key is getting the parent/guardian not to feed the child's dependence. The child must not be allowed to stay home from school if he/she is not ill. The parent/guardian must not come into the building with the child, as this encourages drama. Most parents/guardians are exhausted and willing to accept assistance with the matter.)

CONFLICT RESOLUTION

Purpose:

To resolve school conflicts that cause distress and disrupt class

Suggested Students:

Students who need assistance resolving a conflict

Grades K–5

Materials Needed:

For The Leader:
- ☐ Copy of the *I-Message* poster (page 143)

For The Students:
None

Activity:

(*Note:* Spending time a student who has asked for help resolving a conflict helps the counselor understand the problem and the student's feelings. Open-ended questions can elicit details of the conflict. Students often want to recount only what the other person did. If that's the case, ask, "What would NAME OF OTHER CHILD say about what happened?" This encourages the child to divulge the whole story.)

Ask for details from an adult who refers a student for conflict-resolution assistance. Understanding the general details of the conflict allows you to make sure the session addresses all elements of it. Unfinished business will lead to further conflict.

Once you have a general understanding of the conflict, meet in a private area with thosc involved. Explain that you've called the students together to resolve the conflict. Emphasize that each person will get a turn to talk, that there will be no interrupting or name-calling, and that you're confident the conflict will be resolved. Display the *I-Message* poster and explain that you'll be using *I-Messages* to discuss the conflict.

Ask who would like to begin. If no one volunteers, choose the person who seems most upset. Act as mediator, ensuring that each person gets a chance to talk and that no one interrupts or becomes combative.

The first person gives an *I-Message* to the second person. If the student is having difficulty, say "I feel" to get him/her started. This allows the student to fill in the blank. Most students can proceed from there.

After the first student's *I-Message* is given, look at the second person to indicate that he/she should respond. Remind a student who tries to avoid responding to an *I-Message* that he/she will get a turn to give one, but that this is the time to address the *I-Message* that has been given.

Once the second person has responded, it is his/her turn to give an *I-Message* and the first person's turn to respond. This alternating delivery should continue until all aspects of the conflict have been discussed.

Talk about *apologies* and about how most people feel better once an apology has been made. Ask if anyone wants to say anything else. Most will apologize at this time. Ask:

> ***What will be different from now on?*** (Allow each person to respond.)

Conclusion:

Congratulate the students for resolving the conflict peacefully. Tell them that conflicts with others are normal and can be resolved quickly and peacefully. Encourage the students to use the same steps the next time a conflict arises and to ask for help if they're unable to resolve the conflict by themselves.

If more than two persons are involved in the conflict, follow the same steps. Restrict the meeting to people who are truly part of the conflict. Additional people can make resolving the conflict challenging.

I-MESSAGE

I feel ______________________

when you __________________

____

______________________________.

I want ______________________

____

______________________________.

MESSAGE

THE BEST OF INDIVIDUAL COUNSELING

GETTING ORGANIZED

Purpose:

To help the student understand that poor organizational skills are affecting his/her schoolwork

To teach the student that organizational skills can be learned and new habits can be formed

Suggested Students:

Students who are having difficulty with organizational skills and with completing their work

Grades 2–6

Materials Needed:

For The Leader:

☐ Sample Homework Folder

For The Student:

☐ Folders
☐ Container for school supplies
☐ Backpack
☐ Planner

Preparation:

A student with organizational problems is usually referred by an adult. To gain a good understanding of the problem, discuss the situation with the referring adult. Ask what systems he/she recommends for organizing papers, use of a planner, or keeping track of assignments. Note when the student is expected to record the work. Ask if the teacher would be willing to check the planner or if a peer could assist with the task. If you decide to use a peer, decide who will discuss the job with him/her.

Activity:

Meet with the student to address his/her organizational problems. Ask how he/she views the situation. Use such open-ended statements as:

Tell me about your organizational skills.

Tell me about the inside of your desk and backpack.

Ask how the student keeps track of assignments. Talk about how this affects his/her grades and success in the classroom. Ask:

What do you think you could do differently?

Share the following examples of good organizational skills.

- There are no loose papers in an organized desk.
- In an organized desk, every paper is in a folder. (Show a sample homework folder whose sections are labeled as the teacher requested.)
- Supplies such as glue, crayons, and scissors should be kept in a container.
- You shouldn't have toys at school or in your desk.
- All books should be stacked neatly.

Using the same pointers, talk about how to organize a backpack.

Ask the student about his/her classroom's system for recording assignments in a planner or notebook. (Since you've already discussed this with the teacher, you'll know if the student fully understands what's expected.) If there's no system in place in the classroom, it would be beneficial to help the student develop one.

Help the student get organized. To avoid embarrassment, it's best to do this when other children are not in the room.

Coach the student while he/she empties the desk. If you're not sure where to place papers, put them aside and ask the teacher what to do with them. Encourage the student to throw away trash.

Have the student place his/her papers in folders according to the system the teacher recommends, then place supplies in a sealable plastic bag or other container. If the student doesn't have a container, offer to contact his/her parent/guardian or supply a container yourself.

After the desk is organized, continue coaching while the student organizes his/her backpack.

Once the desk and backpack are clean and organized, discuss a system for recording homework and tests. Remind the student at what time of day he/she is expected to record work in the planner or notebook. Tell the child to have his/her teacher or designated peer check to make sure all items are recorded. Emphasize that this is to help, not punish, the student.

Conclusion:

With the student's permission, let his/her parent(s)/guardian(s) know what you've worked on and elicit their help. Parents/guardians can encourage the child to stay organized and check the planner/notebook. They may consider praising and rewarding good organizational skills.

Tell the student you'll be checking for the next several days to see if his/her desk and backpack stay organized. Let the child know you'll also be asking the teacher about his/her progress. To further encourage compliance, you could set up a reward system. (*Note:* Students often enjoy inviting a friend to have a private lunch in the counselor's office as a reward. This motivates the desired behavior and can also improve social skills.)

TATTLING

Purpose:

To help the student understand the difference between *tattling* and *telling* information that will keep people and property safe

Suggested Students:

Students who have a habit of tattling

Grades K–3

Materials Needed:

For The Leader:
- ☐ Copy of *The Story of Tattling Sue* (page 150)

For The Student:
- ☐ Copy of *Tattling Sue* (page 151)
- ☐ Crayons or markers

Preparation:

A student having difficulty with tattling is usually referred by an adult. Ask the adult for details about the child's tattling: It's beneficial to ask when the child tattles, who he/she usually tattles to and on, and how other children react.

Activity:

To put the student at ease, begin by discussing his/her thoughts about school, his/her teacher, and friends. This will break the ice and gently lead into the discussion on *tattling.*

Once a comfort level is established, say:

> ***Your teacher has noticed that you often tell on others and has asked me to talk with you about that. Do you know what telling on others is called?*** (If the child does not say *tattling*, go ahead and use the word.)

Sometimes it's important to tell the teacher things. Information is helpful if it keeps others safe and keeps property from being damaged. (Give examples of damaging property such as breaking a desk, tearing a towel rack off the restroom wall, or throwing rocks.) ***Lately, though, you've been telling the teacher about actions that don't involve hurting people or damaging things.***

Repeat examples the teacher shared with you. Then say:

Tattling causes another problem. Other students don't like when you tattle on them. How do you think they feel? (Make sure feelings such as anger, sadness, worry, and fear are discussed.)

This reminds me of a story I'd like to read to you. I have a coloring page that goes along with the story. Would you like to color while I read aloud? (If the student responds affirmatively, give him/her a copy of *Tattling Sue* and crayons or markers.)

Read *The Story Of Tattling Sue*. You may need to explain some words in the story as you read.

After reading the story, ask:

At the beginning of the story, why did Sue run and tell the teacher everything? (She thought she was supposed to, and she thought it was fun. She probably liked the attention.)

What are some other ways Sue could get the attention of her teacher and the other kids? (She could work hard in school. She could be friendly. She could ask others if they'd like to play with her. She could share.)

How did the kids in the story feel when Sue tattled on them? (They felt scared and worried that they might get into trouble. They felt angry with Sue and didn't want to be her friend.)

Does the teacher need Sue to report everything that happens? (No. The teacher is really good at seeing what's happening.)

What might the teacher need to be told? (The teacher needs to know if someone is hurt or could get hurt, if someone is being threatened by a bully, or if property is being damaged.)

How will other kids feel about Sue if she stops tattling? (They'll like her and want to be her friends.)

What will the teacher do if Sue forgets and starts to tattle? (The teacher will point to his/her eye. This will remind Sue to ask herself, "Am I tattling or telling something important?")

How could this story help you?

Do you think it would be helpful if the teacher gave a private "eye pointing" signal when you start to tell something? (If the student says he/she would find it helpful, say that you'll help him/her talk about it with the teacher. Otherwise, remind the student that he/she will need to stop and think each time he/she starts to tell the teacher something.)

Give the student time to complete the picture.

Ask if the student has any questions.

Conclusion:

Tell the student you're confident that he/she will do a great job remembering not to tattle and will tell only important information to the teacher.

THE STORY OF TATTLING SUE

Once there was a tattler named Sue.
Who thought she knew just what to do.
To the teacher she would run,
And thought it so much fun
To tell tales on a classmate or two.

Sue would tattle if you dropped your glue.
Sue would tattle if your nose you blew.
She would tattle if you stepped out of line.
She would tattle if your smile didn't shine.
Sue would tattle even if what she told was untrue.

Sue didn't know that when she tattled and told,
Kids would be fearful of getting a scold.
They'd worry that the teacher would be displeased.
This caused them wonder if they had teased.
They stayed away from Sue and treated her cold.

One day, Sue learned an important lesson.
Her tattling had caused her friendships to lessen.
The teacher didn't need Sue to spy.
She could watch the kids with her own two eyes.
Sue's classmates found this new wisdom a blessing.

Sue learned what's important for adults to know.
She learned to keep others safe, to the teacher she must go.
When bullies threaten or property is at stake,
A trip to the teacher she surely must make.
Now others want Sue to play and join in as they grow.

If Sue forgets and to the teacher runs
She's given a signal that is private and fun.
The teacher points to her eye.
To show she doesn't need a spy.
Sue thinks, "Do I tell or keep the friendships I've begun?"

TATTLING
SUE

TRANSITION TO MIDDLE SCHOOL

Purpose:

To help students feel less anxious about starting middle school

Suggested Students:

Students who feel anxious about the transition to middle school

Grade 5

Materials Needed:

For The Leader:

- ☐ Combination lock
- ☐ Middle school schedule/procedures
- ☐ Photographs of the school

For The Student:

- ☐ Copy of *Opening A Combination Lock* (page 154)
- ☐ Written details of middle school schedule/procedures

Preparation:

Contact a representative from the middle school to obtain details about schedules; building layout; lunch, restroom, and break procedures; necessary school supplies; and extra-curricular activities. Prepare a detailed sheet with age-appropriate information. If possible, take photographs of the school. Make sure to get pictures of the inside and outside of the building and of areas new students will visit.

Activity:

Meet with the student who feels anxious about starting middle school.

Say that you'd like to talk about the student's worries. Explain that it's normal to have this feeling. Describe a time when you felt worried—perhaps when you first started working at the school. Ask what about middle school worries the student.

Give the student the information you obtained about the middle school and show him/her the pictures. Answer any questions he/she may have. Then explain that you'd like him/her to practice opening a combination lock. (*Note:* Many transitioning students worry about using a combination lock.)

Give the student the information sheet on opening a combination lock, then demonstrate how to do it. After demonstrating several times, give the student a turn. Talk him/her through the procedure and, if necessary, provide hand-over-hand assistance. An unsuccessful practice session will only add to the child's anxiety. Allow the student to open the lock several times, ensuring that he/she is comfortable with the task.

Ask if the student has any questions. If he/she has questions you can't answer, say you'll check and get back to him/her with the answers.

To make the student feel secure, give him/her the name of someone who works at the middle school.

Conclusion:

Assure the student that he/she will be successful in middle school. Encourage the student to ask an adult for help whenever he/she has a question or needs assistance.

Contact the middle school for answers you can't supply. Invite the student to provide feedback after starting middle school. If the student's anxiety persists, help his/her parent(s)/guardian(s) schedule a visit to the middle school.

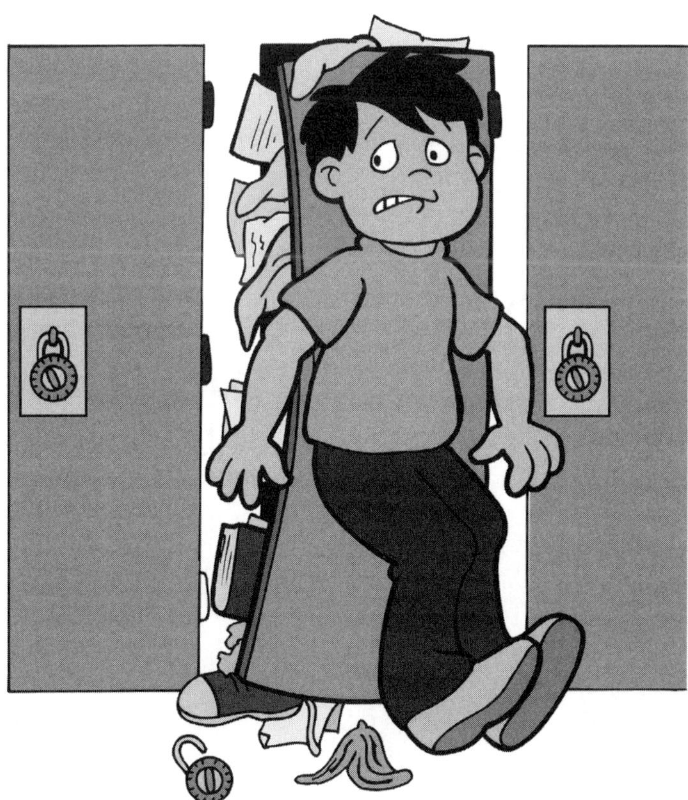

OPENING A COMBINATION LOCK

Clear the lock by spinning the dial clockwise (to the right) a few times.

Stop the dial at the first number in the combination.

Spin the dial counter clockwise (to the left) and stop at the second number in the combination. Make sure you go past the first number before stopping at the second number.

Spin the dial clockwise again. Stop at the third number in the combination.

Pull on the lock to open it.

GRIEF/LOSS

Purpose:

To support students who have suffered a loss or are grieving

Suggested Students:

Students who are grieving the loss of a loved one or pet

Grades K–5

Materials Needed:

For The Leader:

- ☐ Attendance reports
- ☐ Optional: Children's books on grief and loss
- ☐ Computer

For The Student:

- ☐ Copy of *Mandala* (pages 158-160) or drawing paper
- ☐ Crayons or markers

Preparation:

Monitor attendance reports to identify students grieving the loss of a loved one. Tell the office attendants and teachers you need the names of students who may be grieving a loss.

Many students who suffer loss will not request assistance. You may have to seek them out.

Activity:

After learning of a student who has suffered a loss, invite him/her to a private area to discuss the loss. Say:

> ***I've heard that someone special to you has died. I wanted you to know I knew about it. Would you like to talk about it?***

If the student wants to talk, proceed with a session. If the student says he/she doesn't need to talk, tell him/her that's OK. Encourage the student to contact you if he/she has a change of heart. Make sure the student knows how to contact you.

If the student seems uncomfortable talking, offer to read a book on grief. If you have several books on grief, allow the child to choose which book to read.

Another way to encourage the child to talk abut grief is to allow him/her to color. *Mandalas* can be very relaxing. These designs ease tension for some people and may enable the child to talk with less anxiety. Give the child crayons or markers and a copy of a *Mandala* or drawing paper. Free drawing may also comfort the student. You could ask the child to draw a portrait of the person or a picture of the pet that died, a picture showing how the student is feeling, or a scene showing an activity he/she shared with the deceased person.

Have the student tell you about the deceased person or pet. Find out how the child was connected to that person (close family, extended family, friend, family acquaintance, etc.) If the loss is a pet, ask about other pets in the child's home.

Ask about the student's feelings. If he/she has difficulty explaining his/her feelings, you might describe how you felt when you experienced a loss. Tell the student that we often have more than one feeling when dealing with a loss and that all the feelings we have are OK.

To determine how adults in the home are modeling coping skills, ask the student how other family members are dealing with the loss.

If appropriate, discuss funerals:

- If the funeral or visitation has occurred, ask if the student has ever been to a funeral or visitation.
- If the child plans to attend the funeral or visitation, talk about what he/she will see and experience.
- Talk about the body in the casket. Remind the student that the person is not asleep, but deceased.
- Say that many visitors and family members will probably be at the funeral or visitation. Some will be very sad, some a little sad. There may be happy moments. When people die, their loved ones tell stories about them and visit with one another. This is part of the healing process and it is OK.

Tell the student to ask for your help if he/she starts thinking about the loss during the school day. Explain that you'll tell the teacher to call you if the student wishes to talk. If your school district permits, ask the student if it is OK for you to inform his/her parent(s)/guardian(s) that the two of you have met. Otherwise, tell the student that school district policy requires you to inform his/her parent(s)/guardian(s) that you met. You may contact them by phone, send a note home with the student, or mail a letter to the student's home.

Conclusion:

Tell the student you'll check with him/her the following day.

If the student gave permission or your school's policy requires you to do so, contact the parent(s)/ guardian(s) and report on your session. Ask how the child is coping at home. Explain that most children grieve differently than adults. Children may be sad or upset for a few minutes, then become distracted. Ask to be notified of any changes in the child's activity level or demeanor or if any other concerns arise. Say that you'll check on the child the next day and periodically thereafter.

Future sessions may include discussing memories of the deceased, talking about the funeral or visitation, changes that have occurred in the family since the death, and having the child bring pictures of the deceased.

MANDALA

MANDALA

MANDALA

WORRY AND ANXIETY

Purpose:

To help the student deal with anxiety and worries

Suggested Students:

Students referred as a result of anxiety/worrying

Grades K–5

Materials Needed:

For The Leader:

- ☐ Copy of *Sentence Stems* (page 163)
- ☐ Scissors
- ☐ Optional: Stress/anxiety-reducing book for children

For The Student:

- ☐ Paper
- ☐ Crayons or markers

Preparation:

Reproduce and cut apart the *Sentence Stems*.

Activity:

Invite the student to a private area to talk. Explain that you want to get to know him/her a little better and help with any problems he/she may be having.

Ask if the student would like to discuss anything in particular. If so, go with the topic. If no specific issues are mentioned or you have already covered the topic, tell the student you'd like to ask some questions.

Show the student the *Sentence Stems*. Ask if he/she would be willing to finish some sentences for you. Explain that you'll be asking about feelings and, since bodies give clues to feelings, about what the student's body parts do when he/she has those feelings. When we feel happy, for example, we may smile. When we feel sad, we may cry. We may tighten our fists when we feel angry.

Read cards 1–8, pausing for the student's responses. (*Note:* The child may be silent for a while. Some children take longer to process information. And the most revealing information often comes when the child thinks carefully before responding.)

Begin with *Sentence Stem #1*. Read the card to the student. After he/she answers, proceed with cards 2–8. If the student seems puzzled or doesn't answer, give an example.

Reinforce the concept that because our bodies give clues to our feelings, we can use parts of our bodies to help us with our feelings. Emphasize that everyone has feelings and that all feelings are OK.

Discuss what to do with worries, stress, and other unpleasant feelings.

Optional: Present the age-appropriate book you've chosen. Ask if the child would like you to read or wants to do some of the reading. Read the book. Stop, when necessary, to clarify anxiety-reducing techniques.

Practice such anxiety- and stress-reducing techniques as counting to *10,* taking deep breaths, muscle relaxation, walking or exercising, or talking with someone about your feelings. Emphasize that punching someone or destroying property is never a good strategy and that these actions can only cause more anxiety.

Tell the student to picture a stop sign and give him/herself permission to stop whenever he/she begins to worry or feel anxious or stressed.

Give the student drawing paper and crayons or markers. Have him/her draw a stop sign.

Ask the student to close his/her eyes and visualize the stop sign.

Explain that after picturing the stop sign in his/her head, it's time for the student to begin making positive statements that will help him/her feel calmer. Ask:

> ***What positive statements could you say to yourself?*** (If necessary, help the student develop positive statements. Write them on the same piece of paper.)

Read cards 9–12, allowing time for thoughtful answers.

Say:

> ***You now know what situations may cause you to feel worried or anxious. You also know what body clues to watch for, and you have strategies to use when you feel anxious or worried.***

Conclusion:

Say you're confident the student will be able to control his/her worries and anxieties. But remind the student that he/she may always talk with you about school-related anxieties or worries.

SENTENCE STEMS

1. Right now, I feel ____________________.	7. I know I feel __________________, because my _______________________________. (body parts)
2. When I'm at school, I feel ______________.	8. When I'm at home, I feel ______________.
3. When I'm around friends, I feel _________.	9. I feel happy when ____________________. I know this because my body ___________ _________________.
4. I feel sad when _______________________. I know this because my body ___________ _________________.	10. I sometimes feel worried or anxious when _________________________________. I know this because my body___________.
5. I know when I'm worried or anxious, because my body ___________________.	11. When I feel worried or anxious, I can _____ ________________________.
6. I can say positive statements to myself like ___________________________.	12. If I continue to feel worried or anxious, I can talk with ____________________________ about my feelings.

STAYING ON TASK

Purpose:

To help the student improve on-task behavior

Suggested Students:

Students who have difficulty staying on task

Grades K–5

Materials Needed:

For The Leader:

- ☐ Chart of a typical day, broken into small periods of time (prepared by teacher)
- ☐ Sample *My On-Task Behavior Plan* prepared by the student's teacher and counselor (see page 165)
- ☐ Optional: Computer or copy of *My On-Task Behavior Plan,* scissors, and glue

For The Student:

- ☐ Copy of *My On-Task Behavior Plan* (page 167)

Preparation:

Teachers generally refer students who have difficulty staying on task. Talk with the teacher about when the student is off task, what he/she does when off task, and how this affects his/her grades. Ask the teacher for a typical daily schedule broken into small periods of time, according to activities and subjects. This schedule could include:

- arriving and getting settled
- morning seatwork
- calendar
- reading groups
- break
- spelling
- writing
- having lunch

- recess
- science
- social studies
- special classes
- math
- preparing to go home
- independent reading
- dismissal

Ask if the teacher is willing to use a schedule to help the child monitor his/her on-task behaviors and would allow the child to be rewarded for a specified degree of improvement. Explain that as the child improves, expectations of on-task behavior increase and rewards are gradually eliminated. Once you and the teacher reach an agreement, decide whether the teacher or the student should keep the monitoring sheet. Most teachers prefer to keep the sheet themselves.

Before meeting with the student, prepare a behavior plan with the day's periods labeled. Pictures make the chart more appealing and easier for the child to understand. Use your computer to search for clip art to portray each period of time or cut out and paste selected pictures from page 168 onto the chart. See the sample *On-Task Behavior Plan* (below) for ideas.

Activity:

Meet with the student in a private area.

To help the child feel comfortable, ask open-ended questions about friends and school. After a comfort level has been established, explain that his/her teacher has asked you to discuss some classroom problems. Ask:

> ***What kinds of classroom problems do you think we need to discuss***? (This helps you understand if the child is aware of his/her off-task behaviors.)

JOHN'S ON-TASK BEHAVIOR PLAN

Morning Work	Calendar	Reading Groups	Break	Spelling
✔		✔		
Writing	**Lunch**	**Recess**	**Science**	**Social Studies**
✔	✔	✔		✔
Special Classes	**Math**	**Prepare To Go Home**	**Independent Reading**	**Dismissal**
✔	✔ 2x2=?		✔	

I will earn a check at each activity if I stay on task. When I have earned 12 check marks, I will earn a reward.

Reward Choices:

☐ Free Computer Time ☐ Private Lunch With A Friend
☐ Trip To Prize Box ☐ Phone Call Home

If off-task behaviors are not mentioned, say that the teacher has noticed that the student doesn't stay focused on work or responsibilities and that you'd like to help him/her make improvements. Give examples of problem behaviors the teacher mentioned. Then ask the student to tell you about those behaviors.

If the student reports a legitimate reason for those behaviors, such as a classmate talking to him/her during work time, discuss ways to deal with those issues. You could then coach the student on using *I-Messages* to deal with the problem. Or the student could role-play reporting the issue to the teacher.

Tell the student you'd like to help him/her remember to stay on task. If necessary, explain the meaning of the term. Tell the student:

> ***Your teacher and I have broken your day into small periods that you can work on one at a time. This will help you not feel overwhelmed by the whole day. When you can stay on task for a period of time, you'll earn a checkmark for that period. How do you think you'll feel when you earn a checkmark?***

Talk about how proud and relieved the student will feel after completing tasks. Talk about how proud his/her teachers and parent(s)/guardian(s) will feel.

If appropriate, tell the student his/her teacher is willing to offer a reward if he/she really improves. Based on the teacher's recommendation, explain what the student must achieve to earn a reward.

Ask the student what kinds of rewards would motivate him/her. Suggest a private lunch with a friend in the counselor's office, fun time with a friend in the counselor's office, a trip to a prize box, a positive note or phone call home, or a trip to the principal. Allow the student to choose more than one reward.

Show the student the behavior plan with the divided daily schedule. Add the chosen rewards to the bottom of the page. Then ask the student to explain the behavior plan to you. Say that if he/she is successful, more-challenging plans will be substituted until off-task behavior is no longer a problem.

Once the child understands the plan, ask if he/she will allow you to share the plan with his/her parent(s)/guardian(s). Or inform the student that the school district's policy requires you to inform them of the plan. Encourage parent(s)/guardian(s) to motivate the child with positive statements and praise.

Conclusion:

Explain that all the adults involved care about the student and support him/her.

Tell the student you believe he/she can be successful.

Make a copy of the plan for the parent(s)/guardian(s) and several copies for the teacher. Keep a master copy for yourself. Teachers often ask for additional copies.

YOUR NAME

MY ON-TASK BEHAVIOR PLAN

I will earn a check at each activity if I stay on task. When I have earned _____ check marks, I will earn a reward.

Reward Choices:

- ☐ ______________________
- ☐ ______________________
- ☐ ______________________
- ☐ ______________________
- ☐ ______________________
- ☐ ______________________

PICTURES FOR
MY ON-TASK BEHAVIOR PLAN WORKSHEET

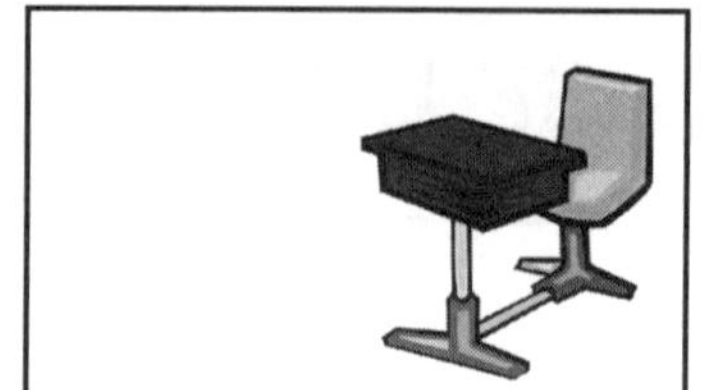

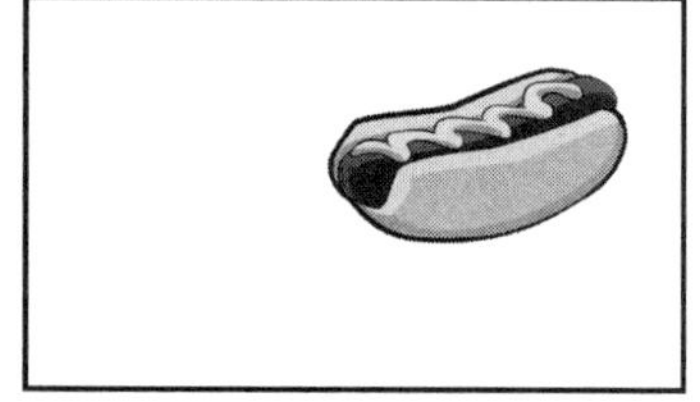

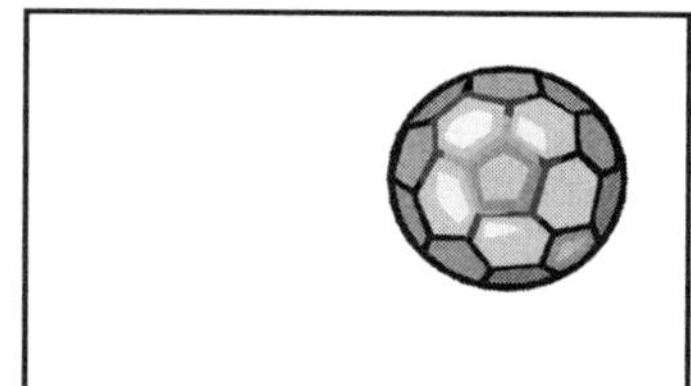

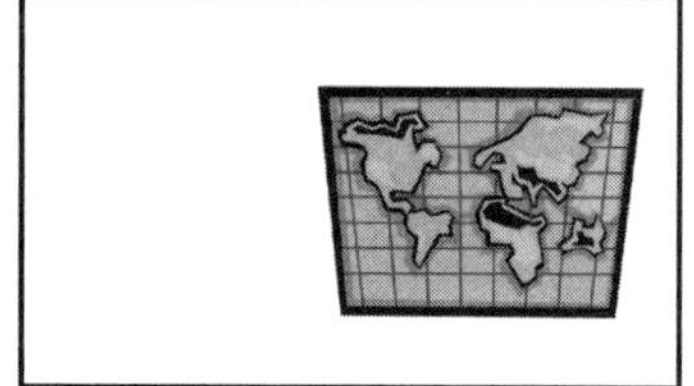

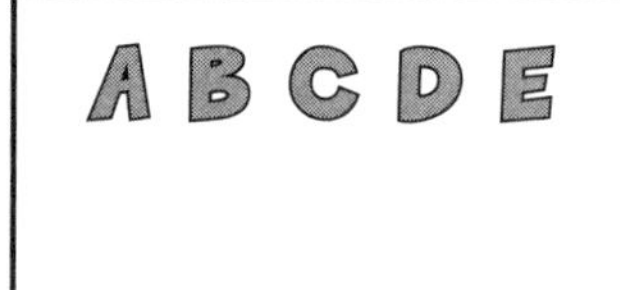

A Note From Marianne Vandawalker

I did regular classroom teaching and served as a reading specialist before going into counseling, so I work with students from a teacher's perspective. I'm aware of the limited time allowed for one-on-one counseling as well as of the teacher's need for a quick resolution to the problem. Getting a student to perform academically, emotionally, and behaviorally are top priorities, since the school's reputation depends on each student's demonstrated improvement.

In counseling, the student is the primary concern. But we can't dismiss the pressure to come up with answers, solutions, and directions that will enable a student in need to succeed. The ideas I've submitted focus on use of efficient counseling situations and short-term reality therapy before referring a student for long-term out-of-school counseling or in-school small-group work.

Issues such as anger management, social skills, loss, and poor academic performance must be addressed at once. Combining child development theories with attentive teacher support, these areas of concern can be explored in a school-counseling situation.

Although designed for written words or sentences, these thinking maps could also be completed by drawing pictures. This same tool can be used to help a student more clearly view his/her problem situation.

Marianne Vandawalker is a retired counselor from North Carolina. She is the author of *Character Fun, Career Fun, What Can I Be?, Study Skills Fun, Year-Round Classroom Games,* and *What Color Are Tears?*

WEBBING

Purpose:

To have the student analyze a problem and its components

Suggested Students:

Students referred because of inappropriate classroom behavior, poor academic progress, and a poor attitude toward school

Grades 1–8

Materials Needed:

For The Leader:
None

For The Student:
- ☐ Copy of *Webbing* (page 172)
- ☐ Pencil

Activity:

Give the student a copy of *Webbing* and a pencil.

Ask:

What do you think your problem is _____________?

Have the student write, inside the large circle, the problem he/she is experiencing. If necessary, help the student write the words.

Help the student identify things that contribute to this problem. Put each detail on a separate line.

Ask the student which of these things are most difficult to control and why. Have the student circle these things.

Ask the student which reasons for the problem can be most easily corrected and why. Have the student put a check mark by each of them.

Ask the student to put a star by one or two checked items.

Help the student list two or three things he/she can do to eliminate the checked contribution(s) to the problem. Be specific. If one reason for the student's poor academic performance is because he/she isn't keeping up with homework assignments, the list might include having a better study space at home or a specific time and amount of time to complete assignments.

Establish a short-term contract for the student to work on the details and report his/her progress in solving the problem.

After dealing successfully with the checked item(s), the student may work on the circled items.

Conclusion:

Review the session by asking what the student has learned.

WEBBING

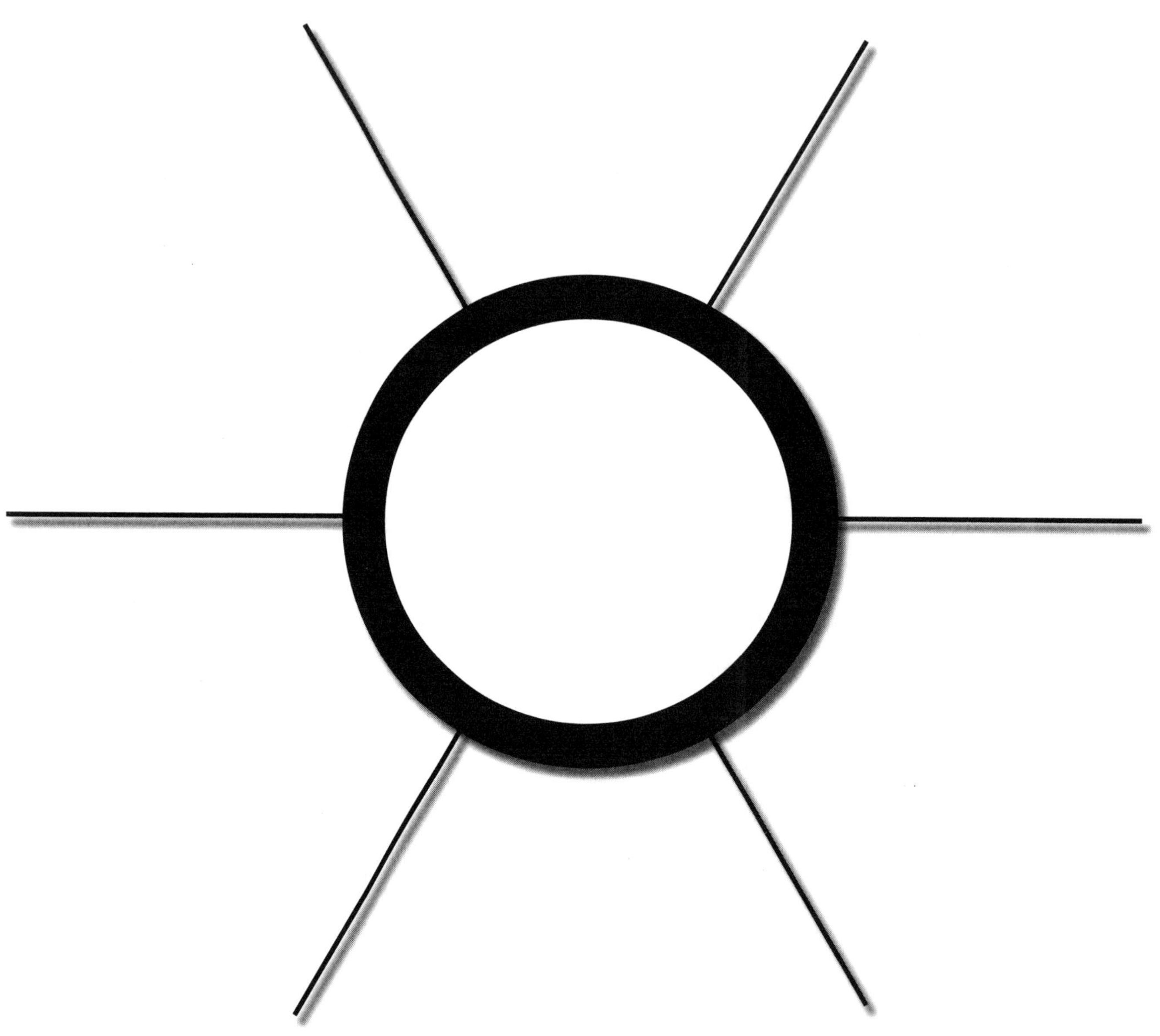

THE BEST OF INDIVIDUAL COUNSELING

SEQUENCE CHAIN VISUAL

Purpose:

To help the student gain a better understanding of what happened

To have the student chronologically list events leading to the problem

Suggested Students:

Students referred as a result of confrontation with another student or with a teacher

Grades K–8

Materials Needed:

For The Leader:
None

For The Student:
- ☐ Copy of *How It All Happened* (page 175)
- ☐ Pencil

Activity:

Give the student a copy of *How It All Happened* and a pencil.

Tell the student to write, in the top rectangular box, a description of the problem that has brought him/her to the counseling office. For example: Nor paying attention in class.

It's important for the student to identify the origin of the problem. Help the student write a description of or illustrate what happen right before he/she got into trouble. Write this in the second rectangular box.

Then ask:

What happened before that?

Continue with this line of questioning until you feel the student has given you as much information as possible and you've reached a starting point.

Help the student list the chain of events that led to him/her being referred to you. Write one event in each box.

For example:

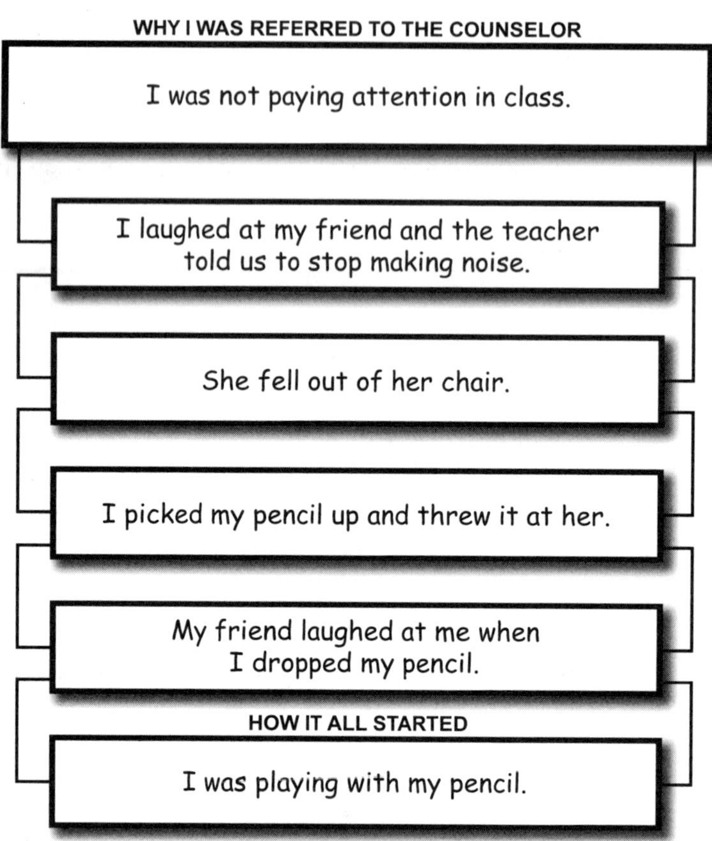

Ask the student to circle the box that describes something he/she could have done differently. Discuss this, then write the new action above the box.

Continue this process until a new approach or an appropriate action is written above the box describing each inappropriate action.

Establish a contract with the student to use the appropriate actions the next time he/she is in a similar situation.

Conclusion:

Review the session by asking what the student has learned. Check on the student's progress at a later time.

HOW IT ALL HAPPENED

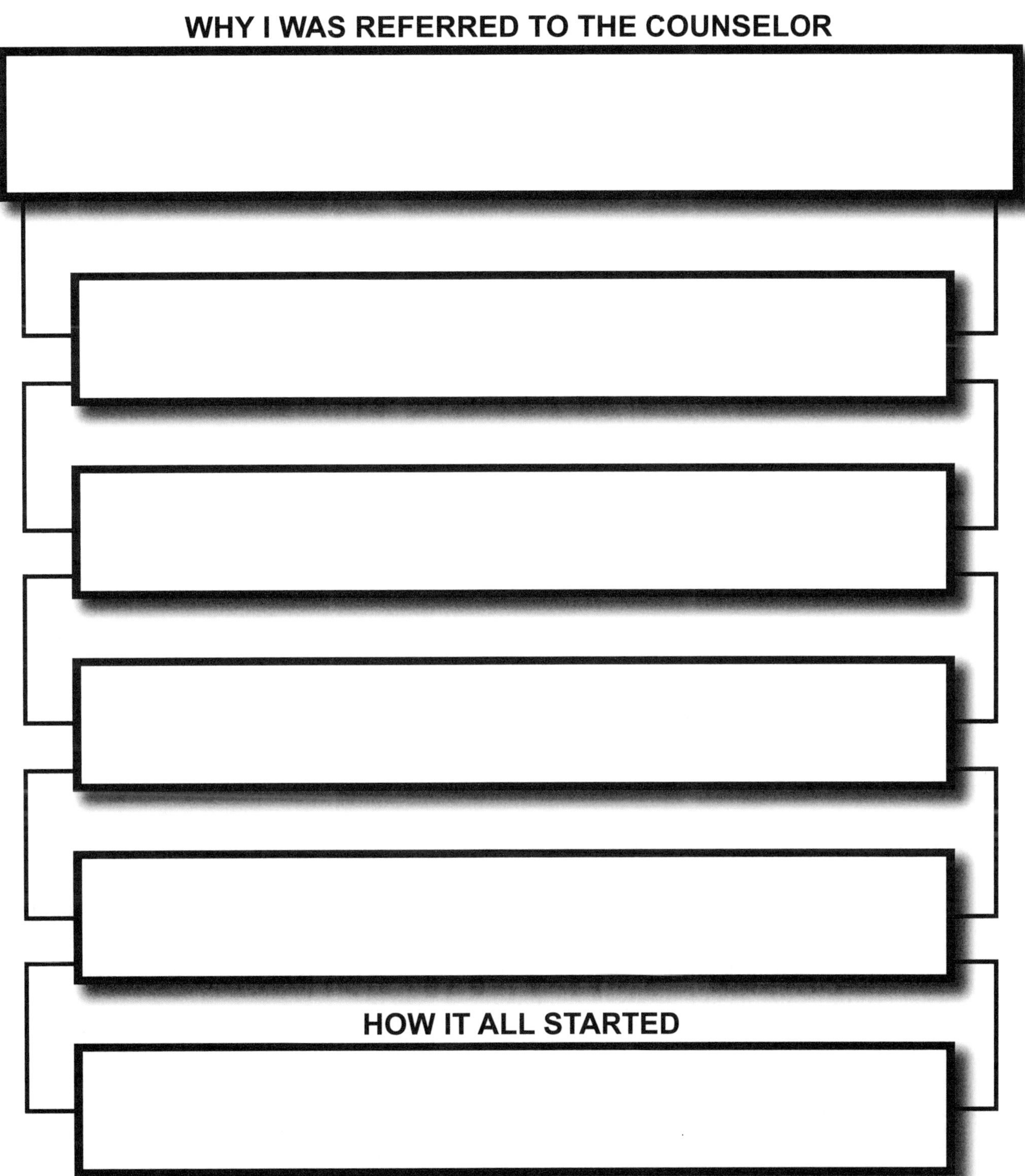

FEELINGS PICTURE

Purpose:

To have the student draw or put into words how he/she feels about something that happened

Suggested Students:

Students referred as a result of inappropriate interaction

Grades K–8

Materials Needed:

For The Leader:

None

For The Student:

- ☐ 2 copies of *Feeling Pictures* (page 178)
- ☐ Pencil

Activity:

Give the student one copy of *Feeling Pictures* and a pencil.

Tell the student to write his/her name in the middle box.

Have the student verbalize the event that has brought him/her to the counseling office.

When the student has finishing describing the event, ask him/her to draw or write his/her feelings about it in each of the four boxes. (*Note:* As the student describes the event, you may ask, "How did you feel about that?" and have the student draw his/her feeling in one of the boxes before continuing. The drawing can be as simple as a happy or sad face.)

Give the student another copy of *Feeling Pictures.*

On this paper, have the student write the name of the person affected by the event.

Help the student describe the affected person's feelings in the four boxes.

Ask the student to circle the boxes that list feelings, such as anger, that could be destructive.

Help the student list what can be done to help heal these feelings.

Establish a short-term contract to guide the student in handling the circled feelings. Under each box, list positive ways to deal with a feeling that might cause a problem if not handled well.

Conclusion:

Review the lesson by asking what the student has learned.

Later, check to see if the student has handled the feelings in positive ways.

FEELING PICTURES

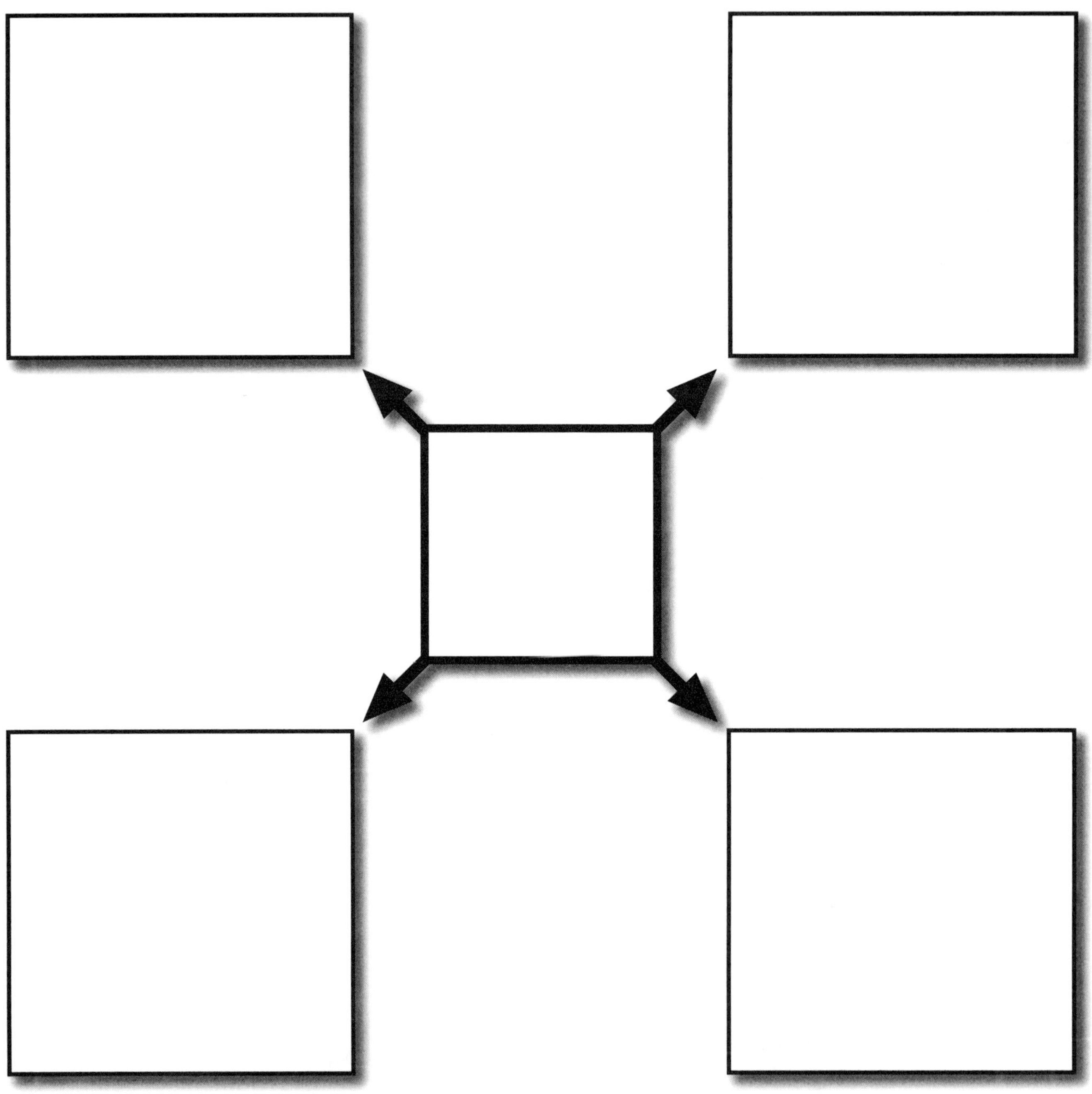

CAUSE AND EFFECT

Purpose:

To have the student identify how the problem interferes with his/her life

Suggested Students:

Students referred as a result of poor academic achievement, poor behavior control, and inappropriate social skills

Grades: 2–8

Materials Needed:

For The Leader:
None

For The Student:
- ☐ Copy of *Cause And Effect* (page 181)
- ☐ Pencil

Activity:

Give the student a copy of *Cause And Effect* and a pencil.

Tell the student to write, in the top rectangular box, a description of the problem that has brought him/her to the counseling office.

Explain that a problem that interferes with someone's life often creates more problems for that person. If the problem is speaking out in class without permission, for example, and the interruptions upset the teacher, additional problems could be things like losing recess time and not getting to play kickball, being sent to the principal's office, upsetting classmates, or being laughed at by other kids.

Help the student describe in writing how the problem interferes with his/her life. These descriptions could include what happens at home and parent(s)/guardian(s) discipline the child. In each of the four circles, write one way the problem interferes with the child's life.

Have the student put a star next to the consequence that would bother him/her most, then draw a picture of that consequence on the back of the paper.

Have the student describe what he/she can do to avoid the unwanted consequence. List these ideas with the picture.

Conclusion:

Ask what the student has learned.

Ask the student to take the visual and report later about how his/her ideas prevented the unwanted consequence. If the ideas are unsuccessful or the student did not follow through with them, schedule another session.

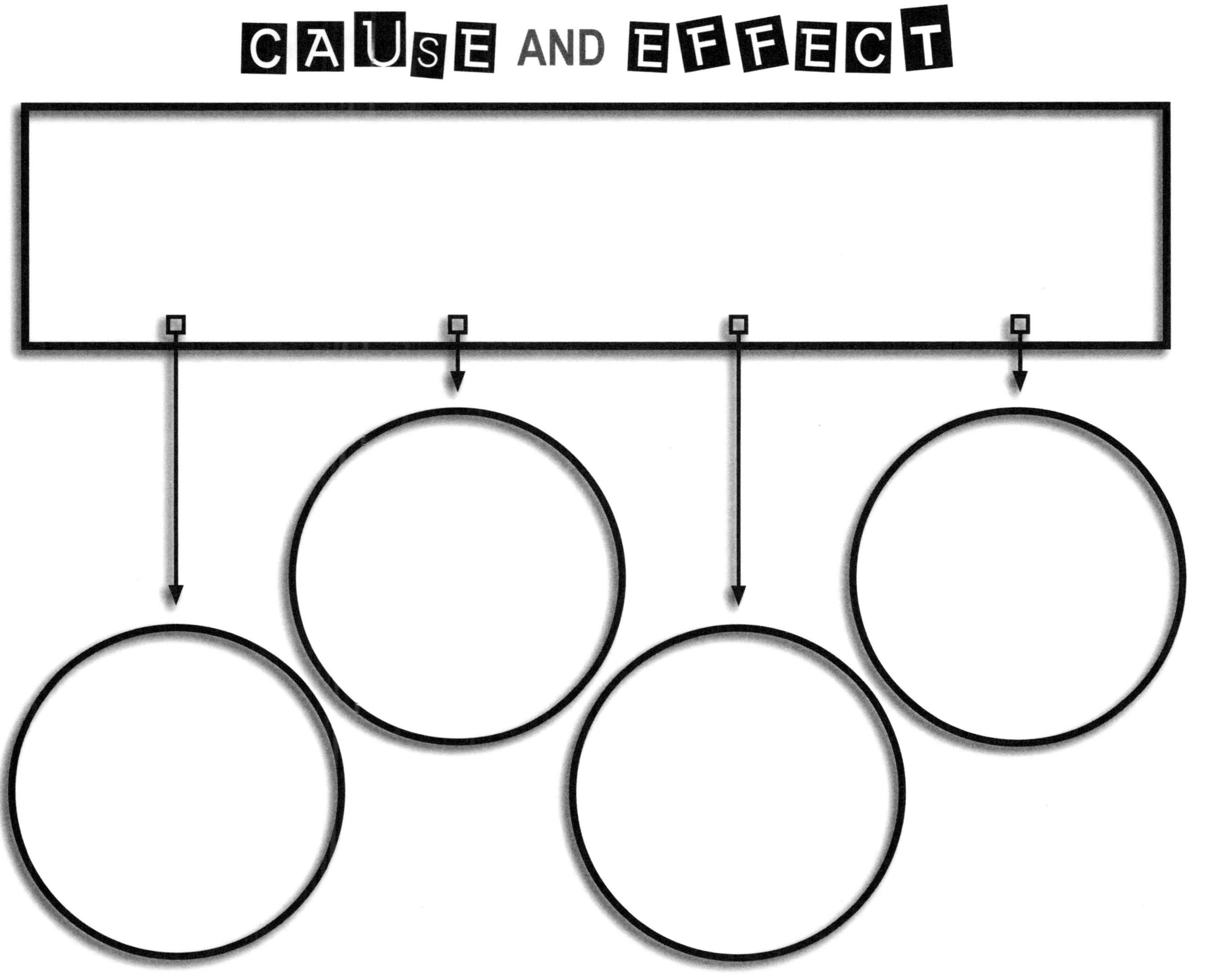
CAUSE AND EFFECT

PROS AND CONS

Purpose:

To have the student identify a problem's pros and cons

Suggested Students:

Students referred as a result of inappropriate behavior, poor social skills, or unsatisfactory academic progress

Grades 2–8

Materials Needed:

For The Leader:
None

For The Student:
- ☐ Copy of *Pros And Cons* (page 184)
- ☐ Pencil

Activity:

Give the student a copy of *Pros And Cons* and a pencil.

In the top left-hand box, tell the student to write a description or draw a picture of the problem that has brought him/her to the counseling office. For example: Not paying attention in class.

Then tell the student to write, in the top right-hand box, a way to solve the problem. For example: Start paying attention.

In the four boxes under the top left-hand box with the plus sign (pro), have the student write the pros of continuing to behave this way. For example: Get attention. Get back at the teacher.

In the four boxes under the top right-hand box with the minus sign (con), have the student write the cons of continuing to behave this way. For example: Getting a bad grade. Not graduating with my friends. Getting into trouble at home.

Have the student check the pro box that most motivates him/her to maintain the attitude/behavior. This suggests why the student acts a certain way in specific situations.

Have the student check the con box that includes the most important reason to discontinue the attitude/behavior.

Conclusion:

Ask what the student has learned.

Encourage the student to remember the pro and con items he/she checked.

Later, check to see if the student has successfully changed his/her attitude/behavior.

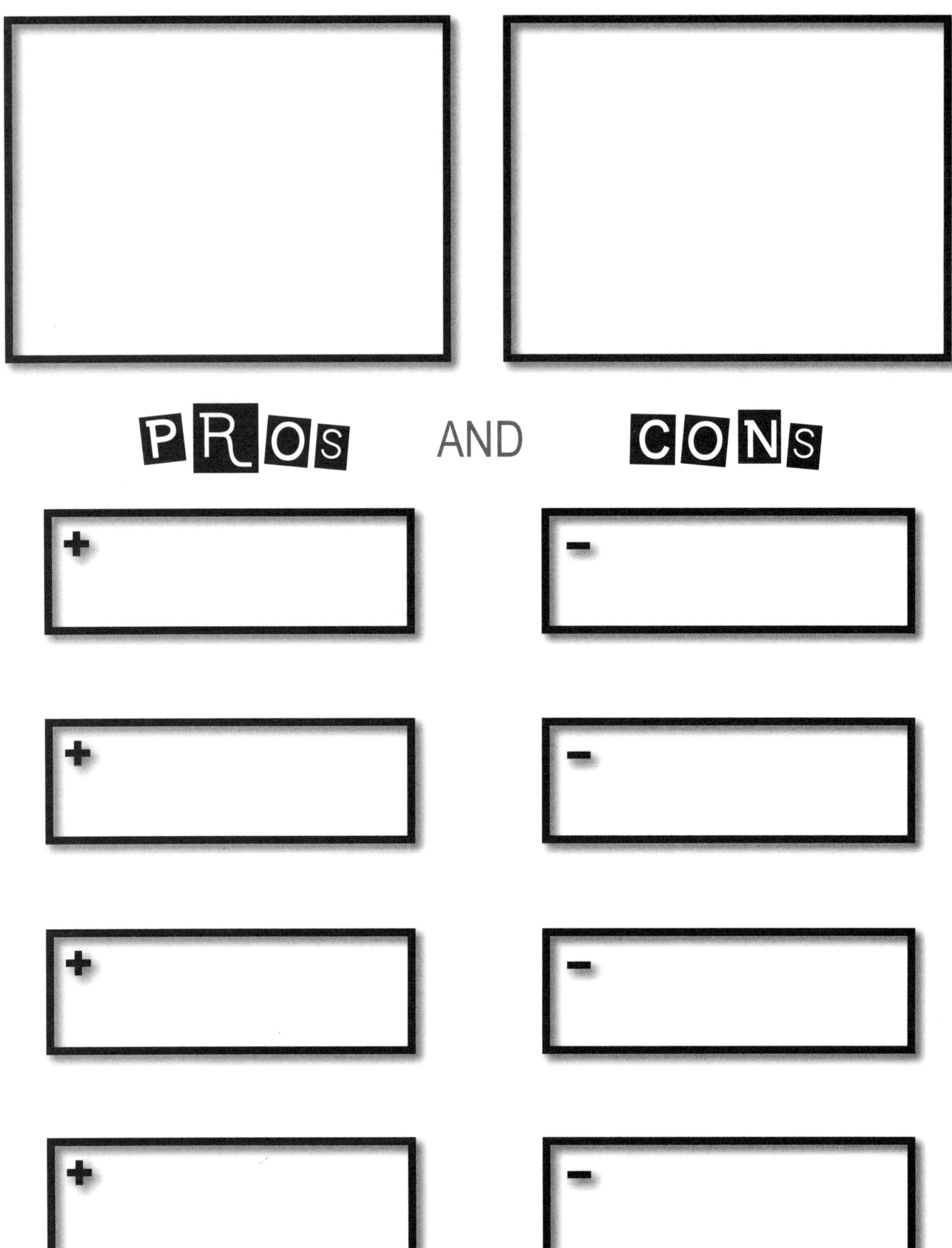
PROS AND CONS
+
−
+
−
+
−
+
−

DIFFERENCES AND SIMILARITIES IN CHOICES

Purpose:

To have the student identify logical and illogical ways of dealing with a problem

Suggested Students:

Students referred as a result of inappropriate behavior

Grades 2–8

Materials Needed:

For The Leader:
None

For The Student:
- ☐ Copy of *Differences And Similarities In Choices* (page 187)
- ☐ Pencil

Activity:

Give the student a copy of *Differences And Similarities In Choices* and a pencil.

In the rectangle at the top of the page, the student should write a description or draw a picture of the problem that has brought him/her to the counseling office.

Ask the student to name the adult or student he/she admires and thinks handles situations appropriately. Write this name next to the word *Choices* on the line above the right-hand circle. For example: Ms. Smith's Choices.

Help the student write a description of one way he/she chose to deal with the problem described on the top line. For example, a student whose problem is not paying attention in class might have chosen to play with a pencil as the teacher gave directions. The choice is written inside the left-hand circle on the first line.

Help the student write, in the right-hand circle, the choice the person he/she admires might make in the same situation. For example, that person might choose to look at the teacher when directions are being given. This choice should be written on the first line inside the right-hand circle.

Have the student look at the two choices, then make a checkmark if his/her choice is the same as the admired person's and an *X* if his/her choice is different. Place this mark on the first line of the intersecting circles. Keep all items within each circle on the same line.

Continue in this manner until all the lines in the circle are filled.

Point out differences and similarities between what the student does in difficult situations and what the admired person does.

Conclusion:

Ask:

How can you act like the person you admire?

What have you learned today?

DIFFERENCES & SIMILARITIES IN CHOICES

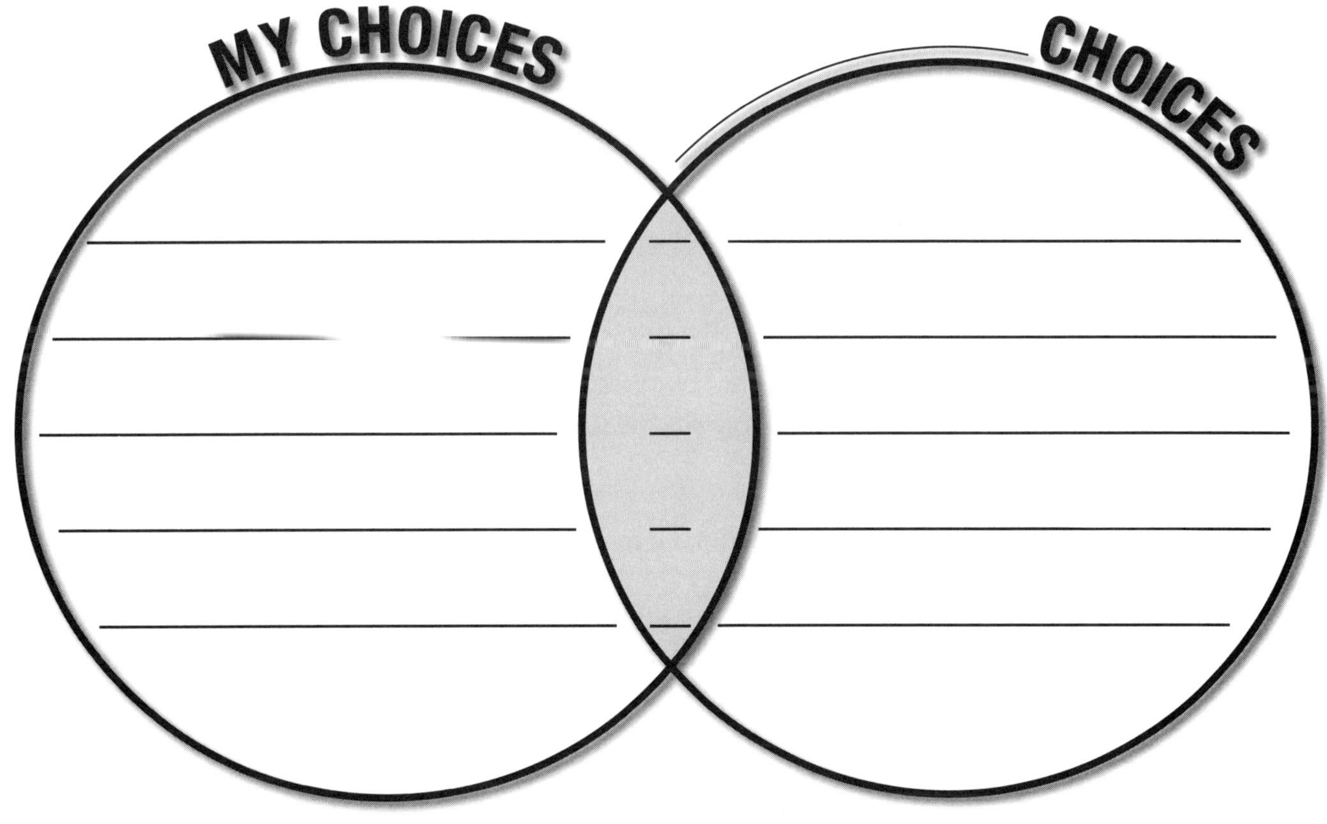

ACTION PLAN

Purpose:

To have the student list details of what he/she will do to correct the problem

To have the student list resources he/she will use to correct the problem

Suggested Students:

Students referred as a result of poor academic performance, poor social skills, inappropriate behavior, and anger-management issues

Grades K–8

Materials Needed:

For The Leader:

None

For The Student:

- ☐ Copy of *Action Plan* (page 190)
- ☐ Pencil

Activity:

Give the student a copy of *Action Plan* and a pencil.

In the large rectangular box, tell the student to write a description or draw a picture of the problem that has brought him/her to the counseling office.

Help the student articulate the steps he/she will take to correct the problem. Write each step in one of the four smaller rectangles.

Help the student write, in each of the four circles, a resource that will help him/her accomplish that step in resolving the problem. A resource could be names of people who can help as well as places, rules, and objects.

Encourage the student to use the listed resource to try to accomplish the first step in resolving the problem.

Conclusion:

Ask what the student learned in this session.

Check later to see if the student successfully followed through on the first step before proceeding to the next step.

ACTION PLAN

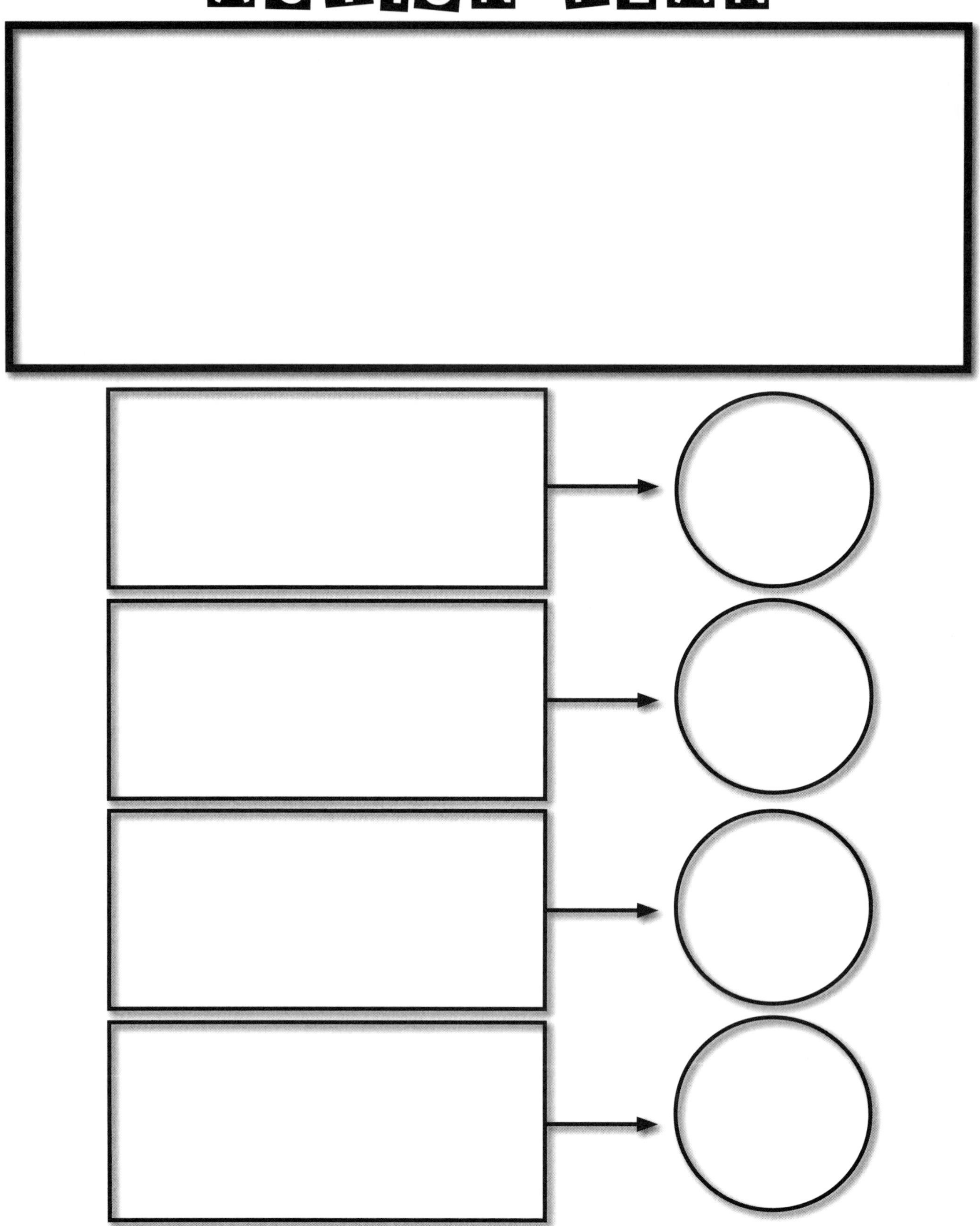

BUILDING TRUST

Purpose:

To enable the counselor to become better acquainted with the student

Suggested Students:

Any referred student

Grades K–8

Materials Needed:

For The Leader:

☐ Optional: Copy of *Building Trust* (page 193)
☐ Optional: Pencil

For The Student:

None

Activity:

Begin by saying:

> ***I have several questions for you. These questions are mostly about the things you like best. I'll be telling you some of the things I like best, too.***

As you discuss the *Building Trust* questions with the student, voice your reactions. This will help build the child's trust in you. Ask the following questions, one at a time, allowing time for the student's reaction and any counselor reaction. (*Note:* If desired, make a copy of *Building Trust* for future reference and write the student's answers on the lines provided.)

> ***What do you like to be called?***
> ***What is your favorite color?***
> ***What is your favorite food?***
> ***What is your favorite book?***
> ***What is your favorite movie?***
> ***What is your favorite TV show?***

What is your favorite car?
What is your favorite sport?
Who is your best friend?
What is your favorite subject in school? Why?
Tell me about your pets and/or your hobbies.
Tell me about your heroes.
What's the best day of the week for you? Why?

Tell the student that you've enjoyed getting to know him/her and that you will try to help solve any problems he/she might have.

Conclusion:

Ask what the student has learned.

BUILDING TRUST

Name ______________________________ Date ____________

What do you like to be called? ______________________________

What is your favorite color? ______________________________

What is your favorite food? ______________________________

What is your favorite book? ______________________________

What is your favorite movie? ______________________________

What is your favorite TV show? ______________________________

What is your favorite car? ______________________________

What is your favorite sport? ______________________________

Who is your best friend? ______________________________

What is your favorite subject in school? ______________________________

Why? ______________________________

____

Tell me about your pets and/or hobbies. ______________________________

____

____

Tell me about your heroes. ______________________________

____

What's the best day of the week for you? ______________________________

Why? ______________________________

____

INTEREST INVENTORY

Purpose:

To explore the student's interests in detail

Suggested Students:

Any referred student

Grades K–8

Materials Needed:

For The Leader:

- ☐ Copy of *Interest Inventory* (page 196)
- ☐ Pencil

For The Student:

- ☐ Optional: Copy of *Interest Inventory* (page 196)
- ☐ Optional: Pencil
- ☐ Optional: Drawing Paper
- ☐ Optional: Crayons or markers

Activity:

Begin by saying:

> ***Today, I want you to tell me about your interests. There are no right or wrong answers.***

Using the *Interest Inventory*, ask one question at a time. Record the student's answers. Feel free to read only the questions that apply to the student. (*Note:* Two optional approaches may be used with this activity. The worksheet can be reproduced for the student, who can write the answers. A student who likes to draw may illustrate his/her answers.)

After completing the *Interest Inventory*, ask:

> ***Which question was the most fun to answer? Why?***
>
> ***Which question was the most difficult to answer? Why?***
>
> ***Which question was most important to you? Why?***
>
> ***What did you learn about yourself today?***

Conclusion:

Thank the student for sharing with you. Repeat a few things you learned to show that you really were listening to the student and were interested in what he/she was saying.

INTEREST INVENTORY

Name ______________________________ Date ____________

If you could make three wishes, what would they be? ______________________________

____

What would you do with $10,000? ______________________________

____

What classes or groups do you especially enjoy? ______________________________

____

If you could be any animal, what animal would you be? ______________________________

Why? ______________________________

Tell me about any talents or skills you have. ______________________________

____

What bugs you most at home? ______________________________

What bugs you most at school? ______________________________

What bugs you most about your friends? ______________________________

What bugs you most about yourself? ______________________________

What do you like best about your best friend? ______________________________

What do you like best about your home? ______________________________

What do you like best about your school? ______________________________

If you could be a character in a favorite movie, which movie would it be? ______________

Why? ______________________________

If you could be a character in a favorite book, which book would it be? ______________

Why? ______________________________

If you could be a character in a favorite cartoon, which cartoon would it be? ______________

Why? ______________________________

If you could take a trip to any place you wanted, where would you go? ______________

Why? ______________________________

If you could write a song about yourself, what would the title be? ______________

What do you worry about? ______________________________

If you were afraid of something or someone, what or who would it be? ______________

What is something I don't know about you? ______________________________

____

IMPORTANT THINGS ABOUT YOU

Purpose:

To ask questions that focus on the student's needs and feelings

Suggested Students:

Any referred student

Grades 3–8

Materials Needed:

For The Leader:
- ☐ Copy of *Important Things About You* (page 199)
- ☐ Pencil

For The Student:
None

Activity:

Begin by saying:

> ***I'm going to ask you to tell me about some situations or events. This will help us get to know each other better.***

Ask the following questions, recording the student's answers on the *Important Things About You Worksheet.*

> ***Tell me something important about yourself.***
>
> ***Tell me who you remember most and why you remember that person.***
>
> ***Tell me about an important event in your life.***
>
> ***What is an important theme or purpose in your life?***

What would you want someone to say about you?

What lessons have you learned in your life?

What rules do you think are important in your life?

After completing the worksheet, ask:

What is the most important thing you told me today? Why was it so important?

What is the least important thing you told me today? Why was it unimportant?

What have you learned today about yourself?

Conclusion:

Thank the student for cooperating and being helpful. After the session, review and analyze the student's answers to better understand his/her interests and feelings.

IMPORTANT THINGS ABOUT YOU

Name ________________________________ Date ____________

Tell me something important about yourself.

____

____

Tell me who you remember most and why you remember that person.

____

____

Tell me about an important event in your life.

____

____

What is an important theme or purpose in your life?

____

____

What would you want someone to say about you?

____

____

What lessons have you learned in your life?

____

____

What rules do you think are important in your life?

____

____

GENERAL INTEREST INVENTORY

Purpose:

To enable the counselor to build a relationship with the student

Suggested Students:

Any referred student

Grades K–8

Materials Needed:

For The Leader:

- ☐ Copy of *General Interest Inventory* (page 201)
- ☐ Pencil

For The Student:

None

Activity:

Begin by saying:

> ***I'm going to ask you to complete some sentences about how you feel. What feelings do you know about?*** (Elicit answers such as *happiness, sadness, loneliness,* or as many feelings as the student can identify.)

Read the sentence starters. Record each response on the *General Interest Inventory*. Feel free to explore with the student any response that requires clarification. Read only the sentence starters that apply to the student.

Conclusion:

After completing the worksheet, ask:

> ***Now that you've given your answers, how do you feel?***
>
> ***What did you learn about yourself today?***

After the session, review and analyze the student's answers to better understand his/her feelings.

GENERAL INTEREST INVENTORY

Name ______________________________ Date __________

FEELINGS

1. I feel ______________________________.
2. I get angry when ______________________________.
3. I feel bad when ______________________________.
4. I'm afraid when ______________________________.
5. I feel I'm at my best when I ______________________________.
6. I feel proud of myself when ______________________________.
7. I often worry about ______________________________.
8. I feel guilty about ______________________________.

SCHOOL

1. School is ______________________________.
2. I wish teachers ______________________________.
3. Going to college is ______________________________.
4. I think books ______________________________.
5. On weekends, I ______________________________.
6. I'd rather read than ______________________________.
7. I think homework ______________________________.
8. When I finish high school, I ______________________________.
9. When I take my report card home, ______________________________.
10. I don't know how to ______________________________.
11. I would like to be ______________________________.
12. When I read out loud, ______________________________.
13. I think studying ______________________________.
14. I wish I could ______________________________.
15. I'd read more if ______________________________.

FAMILY

1. I wish my mother ______________________________.
2. My brothers/sisters ______________________________.
3. I wish my father ______________________________.

FRIENDS

1. I look forward to ______________________________.
2. I wish my friends wouldn't ______________________________.
3. I like to be with my friends when ______________________________.
4. My friends think I ______________________________.
5. My idea of a good time with my friends is ______________________________.

SELF-AWARENESS

Purpose:

To learn more about how a student feels about him/herself and others

Suggested Students:

Any referred student

Grades 3–8

Materials Needed:

For The Leader:
- ☐ Copy of *Self-Awareness* (pages 203-204)
- ☐ Pencil

For The Student:

None

Activity:

Begin by saying:

> ***I'll be asking how you feel about different situations. You may answer with* Yes *or* No. *Your answers will help me understand how you feel inside. There are no wrong answers.***

Read the statements on the *Self-Awareness Worksheet.* Encourage the student to say the first thing that comes to mind.

Conclusion:

After the session, review the answers recorded on the worksheet to determine how the student seems to feel about him/herself. Use your analysis as a springboard for future discussions with the student.

SELF-AWARENESS

Name ______________________________ Date ____________

SCHOOL

1.	Classmates make fun of me.	Yes	No
2.	I am smart.	Yes	No
3.	When the teacher calls on me, I get nervous.	Yes	No
4.	Tests make me nervous.	Yes	No
5.	I have good ideas in class.	Yes	No
6.	I'm good at schoolwork.	Yes	No
7.	I'm slow in finishing my classwork.	Yes	No
8.	I'm slow in finishing my homework.	Yes	No
9.	I daydream in class.	Yes	No
10.	I'm important in class.	Yes	No
11.	I'm a good reader.	Yes	No
12.	I can't remember what I've learned.	Yes	No

SELF-IMAGE

1.	I'm a good person.	Yes	No
2.	I'm different from other people.	Yes	No
3.	I would rather work by myself than in a group.	Yes	No
4.	I'm a leader in group activities.	Yes	No
5.	I have many friends.	Yes	No
6.	I like the way I am.	Yes	No
7.	I feel left out of things.	Yes	No
8.	I'm unpopular.	Yes	No
9.	I'm upset about my looks.	Yes	No
10.	I have pretty eyes.	Yes	No
11.	I like my hair.	Yes	No
12.	I wish I were different.	Yes	No
13.	I'm good-looking.	Yes	No

BEHAVIORS

1.	I cry easily.	Yes	No
2.	I think inappropriate thoughts.	Yes	No
3.	I can be trusted.	Yes	No
4.	I lose my temper easily.	Yes	No
5.	I'm easy to get along with.	Yes	No
6.	I'm clumsy.	Yes	No
7.	I sleep well at night.	Yes	No
8.	I'm among the last chosen for games.	Yes	No
9.	I'm mean to others.	Yes	No
10.	I'm cheerful.	Yes	No
11.	I have lots of energy.	Yes	No
12.	People pick on me.	Yes	No
13.	I'm obedient at home.	Yes	No
14.	I'm obedient at school.	Yes	No
15.	I often get into trouble.	Yes	No
16.	I'm usually nervous.	Yes	No
17.	I behave badly at home.	Yes	No
18.	I do bad things.	Yes	No
19.	I'm unpopular.	Yes	No
20.	I behave well in school.	Yes	No
21.	I usually want my own way.	Yes	No
22.	I give up easily.	Yes	No
23.	It's hard for me to make friends.	Yes	No

COMMENTS:

WHAT BUGS YOU?

Purpose:

To help the student discover situations in which he/she reacts negatively

Suggested Students:

Students who have anger-management or conflict issues

Grades 4–8

Materials Needed:

For The Leader:

- ☐ Copy of *What Bugs You?* (page 207)
- ☐ Pencil

For The Student:

None

Activity:

Begin by saying:

> ***Sometimes things happen that really bother us. I am going to read four situations. If any of these situations would bother you, tell me why and what you usually do when it happens. There are not necessarily right or wrong answers, but some responses may be more appropriate than others. We'll talk about that.***

Ask the questions and record the student's answers on the activity sheet. Begin with the *Yes* and *No* questions, then probe for further information with the *Why* and *What would you usually do?* questions.

After completing the worksheet, ask:

Which situation seems to be a problem for you? Why or how?

In which situation do you think you reacted in an inappropriate way? Why?

In which situation do you think you reacted in an appropriate way? Why?

What have you learned today?

Conclusion:

After the session, review the worksheet to gain insight into the student's thinking.

WHAT BUGS YOU?

Name ______________________________ Date ____________

Would it bug you if you failed at something? **Yes** **No**

Why? What do you usually do if you fail at something?

____

____

____

____

Would it bug you if you thought you looked stupid to others? **Yes** **No**

Why? What do you usually do if you think you look stupid to others?

____

____

____

____

Would it bug you if others made fun of you? **Yes** **No**

Why? What do you usually do if others make fun of you?

____

____

____

____

Would it bug you if you weren't invited to go with your friends? **Yes** **No**

Why? What do you usually do if you aren't invited to go with your friends?

____

____

____

____

____

____

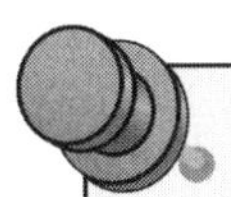

A Note From Pat Vargas

My entries for this book focus on a writing theme because:

- Writing can help the student articulate feelings, images, and thoughts that might remain outside his/her conscious awareness.
- Writing gives the leader insight into the student's thoughts, use of words, and verbal and written fluency.
- Writing allows the student to express him/herself without inhibitions that may exist when speaking.
- Writing can enhance a student's self-awareness.

When using writing as a counseling tool, begin with items that interest the student and that make the activity enjoyable.

Pat holds a B.S. in elementary education, a master's in education, and a master's in counseling (K–12). She holds kindergarten, gifted/talented, reading specialist, and bilingual certifications. Pat became a certified Character Counts! national trainer and traveled the nation training groups in character education. She retired in May 2001 and is currently a field specialist for the alternative certification program for the Region 19 Educational Service Center in El Paso. She and her husband have three grown children and four grandchildren: Alex, Maddie, Charlotte, and Evelyn.

Pat is the author/coauthor of *Alex and Maddie, Character Dominoes, Character Cards,* and *Character Cookies.*

JUST ME! BOX

Purpose:

To encourage positive *I-Statements*

To emphasize building healthy self-esteem and personal worth

Suggested Students:

Students referred as a result of low self-esteem and/or withdrawn behavior

Grades K–5, Orally For Grades K–1

Materials Needed:

For The Leader:

- ☐ Various art materials—sticky notes, magazines, scissors, markers, colored paper, lined paper, glue, crayons

For The Student:

- ☐ Stickers, pictures, sayings, quotes, other items that reflect the student's interests or identity
- ☐ Small box or shoe box
- ☐ Glue
- ☐ Scissors
- ☐ Paper
- ☐ Pencil

Preparation:

Prior to the lesson, instruct the student to collect stickers, pictures, sayings, quotes, and other items that reflect his/her interests or identity and bring them to the meeting.

Activity:

Set out a selection of art materials. Give the student a box, scissors, and glue.

Tell the student he/she is going to make a *Just Me! Box* and decorate it with the items he/she brought to the session and other art materials.

Give the student paper and a pencil. Have the student write something positive about him/herself and put the paper into the box. Each time the student comes for counseling, have him/her add to the box by writing something positive about him/herself. (*Note:* If you're working with a K–1 student, write his/her positive statements, then place the paper in the box.) Examples could be:

- I'm a good friend.
- My teacher says I'm working harder in class.
- I like myself.
- I helped my little brother/sister with homework last night.

The student could also bring positive notes from parents, siblings, friends, and/or teachers to add to the *Just Me! Box*.

Conclusion:

When you've completed all the sessions, the *Just Me! Box* should be full of positive statements the student may review when he/she has a bad day.

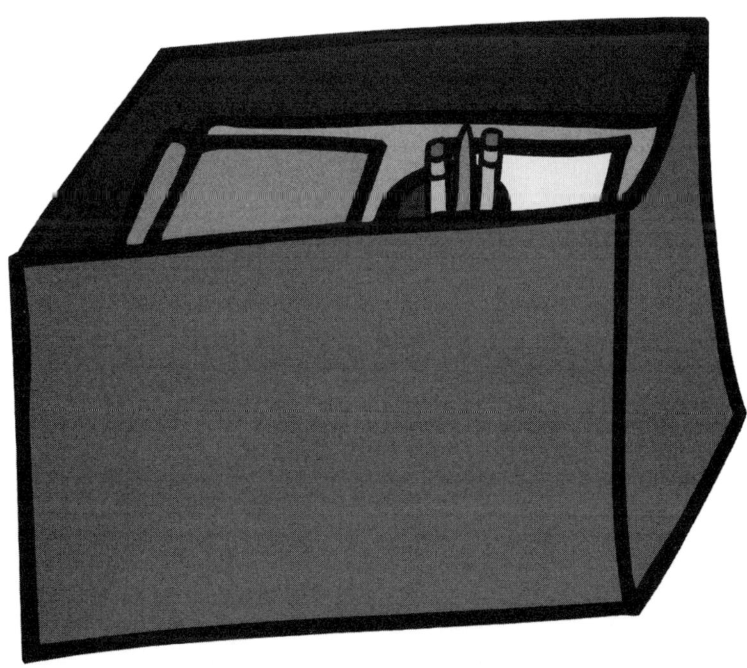

MY FEELINGS/THOUGHTS DIARY

Purpose:

To emphasize the importance of talking about feelings

To help students realize that talking about feelings and thoughts increases the likelihood that their concerns will be addressed and their needs will be met

Suggested Students:

Students referred as a result of aggressive or withdrawn behaviors and students who have experienced a traumatic event such as loss of a family member and/or friend

Grades 2–5

Materials Needed:

For The Leader:

- ☐ Optional: Stapler and staples
- ☐ Various art materials—sticky notes, magazines, scissors, markers, colored paper, lined paper, glue, crayons

For The Student:

- ☐ A blank notebook or loose-leaf paper and two sheets of colored construction paper
- ☐ Pencil

Preparation:

If you're not using a blank notebook, obtain loose-leaf paper and two sheets of colored construction paper. Place the paper inside the construction paper and staple everything together to form a notebook.

Activity:

Set out a selection of art materials.

Give the student a blank notebook or one made of construction paper and loose-leaf paper and a pencil.

Have the student make a daily entry stating how he/she felt that day. It may be written or drawn at the top of the page. The student should include important feelings or thoughts he/she had during the day. Ask the student to write descriptions or draw or cut out pictures of things that happened to cause those feelings or thoughts. The student may make this entry during a counseling session or at another time.

Have the student keep the diary for at least 10 school days. Encourage him/her to also make entries on the weekend. After the initial period, entries maybe made less frequently.

Conclusion:

After each entry or session, allow the student to voice his/her feelings, then discuss them.

Extensions: Ask the student to make an entry after a bad day, in anticipation of a special occasion, prior to upcoming stressful events (testing, medical exams, etc.), holidays, vacations, birthdays, etc. You may also ask the student to make entries weekly or at other regular intervals.

CHOICES, CHOICES, CHOICES

Purpose:

To have the student choose between two completely different selections

To have the student examine his/her feelings and thoughts

Suggested Students:

Students referred as a result of impulsive behaviors and/or inappropriate responses

Grades 2–5

Materials Needed:

For The Leader:

None

For The Student:

- ☐ Copy of *Choices, Choices, Choices* (page 215)
- ☐ Pencil

Activity:

Give the student a copy of *Choices, Choices, Choices* and a pencil.

Tell the student to read each question, then circle his/her response. You may have to read some choices to the student.

Have the student clarify the reasons for his/her choices.

Conclusion:

Thank the student for his/her cooperation and emphasize some choices for which the student was able to give good reasons.

(*Note:* You may focus on the descriptors/choices you feel might give more insight into the student. You may expand this activity into 1–4 days, depending on how many descriptors/choices you want to cover in one session.)

Extension: These choices may be written or illustrated in the student's daily journal.

CHOICES, CHOICES, CHOICES

Name______________________________________ Date ______________

I am:

1.	more like a	cat	dog
2.	more like a	weed	rose
3.	more often	right	wrong
4.	more like a	bike	roller skate
5.	more like an	apple	orange
6.	more often	alone	with friends
7.	more like a	pencil	crayon
8.	more like a	follower	leader
9.	more like a	hare	tortoise
10.	more like a	bat	ball
11.	more like	light	darkness
12.	more	happy	sad
13.	more like a	picture	frame
14.	more like a	computer	television
15.	more like a	number	letter
16.	more like a	soccer ball	tennis ball
17.	more like a	window	door
18.	more like a	stove	refrigerator
19.	more like a	friend	enemy
20.	more like	ice cubes	warm water

POSITIVE THOUGHTS DIARY

Purpose:

To emphasize the power of positive thinking

Suggested Students:

Students referred because of low self-esteem and/or withdrawn behavior

Grades 2–5

Materials Needed:

For The Leader:

- ☐ Optional: Stapler and staples
- ☐ Various art materials—sticky notes, magazines, scissors, markers, colored paper, lined paper, glue, crayons

For The Student:

- ☐ Blank notebook or loose-leaf paper and two sheets of colored construction paper
- ☐ Pencil

Activity:

Give the student a blank notebook. Or have the student make a notebook by folding the construction paper in half, placing the lined paper inside, and stapling the materials together. Give the student a pencil.

Have the student decorate the notebook with the art supplies, then title it *Positive Thoughts Diary.*

Inform the student that all entries in this diary must be positive. Ask him/her to make the first entry, then discuss what the student wrote.

Conclusion:

Have the student make additional entries at each counseling session or another time. Discuss each entry with the student.

Extension: Continuing to emphasize the importance of positive thoughts, have the student illustrate the diary entries. Have the student take the completed diary home to share with his/her parent(s)/ guardian(s).

INSTANT REPLAY

Purpose:

To provide an opportunity for the student to recall/reassess prior communications with peers

Suggested Students:

Students referred because of impulsive behaviors and/or inappropriate responses

Grades 2–5

Materials Needed:

For The Leader:
None

For The Student:
- ☐ Copy of *Instant Replay* (page 218)
- ☐ Pencil

Activity:

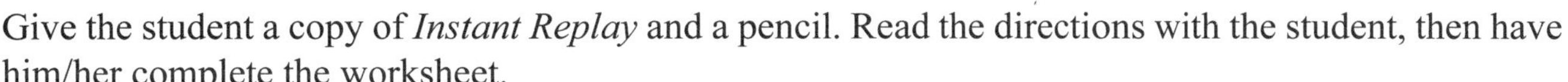

Give the student a copy of *Instant Replay* and a pencil. Read the directions with the student, then have him/her complete the worksheet.

Using the statements on the completed worksheet, reflect on what the student initially said or did and how he/she would now react/respond.

Conclusion:

Tell the student to let you know when an event listed on the worksheet occurs again. Explain that you'll ask if he/she handled the situation differently, learning from prior mistakes.

INSTANT REPLAY

Name ________________________________ Date ____________

Sometimes we say or do something we really don't mean. If an instant replay were possible, what would you say or do differently? Write down what someone said or did, what you said or did, and what you would say or do today.

Someone said or did: ________________________________

____

____

____

____

I said or did: ________________________________

____

____

____

____

Today, I would say or do: ________________________________

____

____

____

____

____

UNDERSTANDING ME

Purpose:

To allow the student to discover and explore some of his/her likes, dislikes, interests, fears, attitudes, goals, etc.

Suggested Students:

Students referred because of low self-esteem, withdrawn behaviors, and/or negativity toward certain people or activities

Grades 2–5

Materials Needed:

For The Leader:

None

For The Student:

- ☐ Copy of *Understanding Me* (page 220)
- ☐ Pencil

Activity:

Give the student a copy of *Understanding Me* and a pencil.

Have the student read and complete each sentence. (*Note:* If the student has difficulty writing the answers, read each sentence aloud and record his/her responses on the worksheet.) Have the student elaborate on his/her responses.

If time allows, have the student illustrate a few of his/her responses. You might suggest that the student illustrate the activities that seem most problematic to him/her.

Conclusion:

Collect the worksheet and review the student's responses for further counseling direction.

Extension: After completing the worksheet, have the student categorize each answer as a good or bad feeling. Have him/her print *G* before a statement that describes a good feeling and *B* before a statement that describes a bad feeling. Focus on discussing the responses the student has indicated describe a bad feeling.

UNDERSTANDING ME

Name ________________________________ Date __________

My favorite subject in school is ______________________________.

The kind of teacher I like best is ______________________________.

My saddest days are when ______________________________.

I get into trouble when I ______________________________.

My favorite sport is ______________________________.

When my team is losing, I ______________________________.

My feelings can be hurt when ______________________________.

I'd like to tell my parents that ______________________________.

I laugh when ______________________________.

I need improvement in ______________________________.

I'd like to tell my best friend that ______________________________.

On vacations with my family, I like ______________________________.

My favorite food is ______________________________.

I'm most afraid of ______________________________.

When I see an argument, I ______________________________.

If I saw someone doing something dishonest, I would ______________________________.

When my friends and I get together, ______________________________.

When I don't understand a lesson in class, I ______________________________.

When I have trouble doing my homework, I ______________________________.

When someone hurts me, I ______________________________.

The happiest day of my life was when ______________________________.

Success means ______________________________.

Failure means ______________________________.

I cry when ______________________________.

My parents think I'm ______________________________.

My friends think I'm ______________________________.

I consider it dishonest to ______________________________.

I'm uncomfortable when ______________________________.

I get angry when ______________________________.

My goal in school is to ______________________________.

My goal in life is to ______________________________.

WHAT WILL I PACK?

Purpose:

To have the student choose which items and possessions are most important to him/her

Suggested Students:

Students referred because of low self-esteem, poor decision-making skills, and/or inability to express feelings and needs

Grades 2–5

Materials Needed:

For The Leader:
None

For The Student:
- ☐ Copy of *What Will I Pack?* (page 222)
- ☐ Pencil, crayons, or markers

Activity:

Give the student a copy of *What Will I Pack?* and a pencil, crayons, or markers.

Instruct the student to write or draw, in the picture of the duffle bag, the items most important to him/her. Emphasize the need to be selective, because the amount of space in the bag is limited.

Discuss the student's choices and clarify the reasons for each. (*Note:* You may focus on the choices you feel might give more insight into the student. You may expand this activity into 1–4 days, depending on how many descriptors/choices you want to cover in one session.)

Conclusion:

Compliment the student's choices and the reasons he/she used to clarify them.

Extension: These choices may be illustrated in the student's daily journal. You may ask the student to share these choices with his/her parent(s)/guardian(s).

WHAT WILL I PACK?

Directions: Pretend you're going to take a long trip to a faraway land. You may carry only what fits into your duffle bag. Draw or write, in the duffle bag, those items you wish to take.

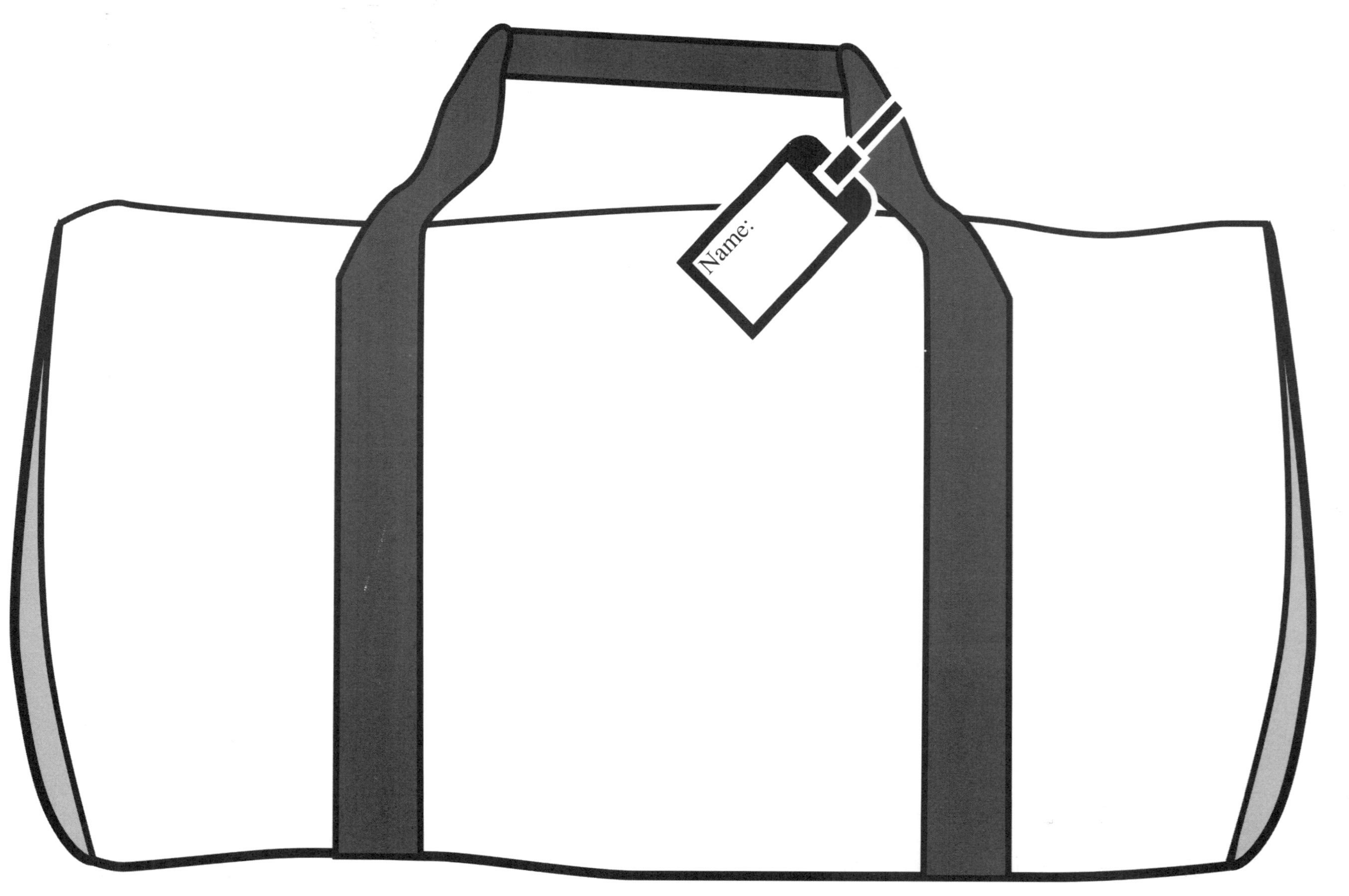

MY SPECIAL GIFT BOXES

Purpose:

To give the student the opportunity to evaluate his/her feelings and thoughts

Suggested Students:

Students referred because of poor decision-making skills, inappropriate responses, and poor social skills

Grades K–5

Materials Needed:

For The Leader:
None

For The Student:
- ☐ Copy of *My Special Gift Boxes* (page 224)
- ☐ Pencil, crayons, or markers

Activity:

Give the student a copy of *My Special Gift Boxes* and a pencil, crayons, or markers.

Tell the student to read the question under each gift box, then draw or write his/her response.

Discuss the student's choices and clarify the reasons for each choice. You may choose to first discuss the gift boxes which might give you more insight into the student. (*Note:* You may expand this activity to 1–4 days, depending on how many choices you want to cover in one session.)

Conclusion:

Compliment the student's choices and the reasons he/she used to clarify them.

Extension: As you discuss each response, the student may cut out the gift box and glue it into his/her daily journal. He/she may elaborate on each *Special Gift Box* in later journal entries.

MY SPECIAL GIFT BOXES

What would you put in the *Special Gift Box* for your best friend?

What would you put in the *Special Gift Box* for yourself?

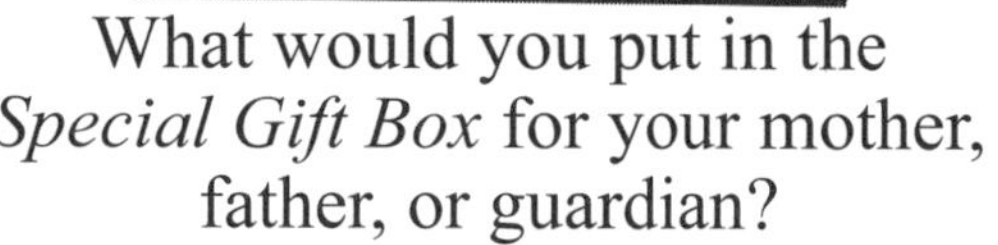

What would you put in the *Special Gift Box* for your mother, father, or guardian?

What would you put in the *Special Gift Box* for the poor people in your city?

A Note From Debra Wosnik

A colleague and I recently agreed that it's difficult to prepare for individual counseling sessions and admitted we feel like we're always flying by the seat of our pants. Although counselors see similar situations, each individual is different and each student's problems are unique. Family backgrounds, ages, and personalities vary. Planning and preparing for groups and class lessons is much easier.

On the first day of school, I have no students to counsel. By the end of the school year, I've usually advised 75 students. This year set a record at my 1150-student, year-round school: I've seen 80 children. I feel like seeing each one for 10 minutes is all I can do and that preparing something great is more than I can do. I'm excited about this book, because I need all the ideas I can get. The ideas I've suggested are simple and have been effective with my students.

Debra Wosnik is a counselor in Utah and the author of *Life Isn't Always Fair* and *The I Hate Wendy Club.*

FIELD TRIP

Purpose:

To have the students visit a college campus

Suggested Students:

Students referred for making choices that will limit their academic and social success

Grades 5–6

Materials Needed:

For The Leader:

None

For The Student:

- ☐ Copy of *Parental Permission Slip* (page 228)
- ☐ Copy of *Teacher Permission Slip* (page 229)
- ☐ Comfortable shoes

Preparation:

Select a few at-risk students who have completed their work for two weeks or who have had two weeks without a behavior incident. Get your principal's permission to take the students to visit a college campus. Then call a local college to arrange to visit the campus and a class the students would like to attend. (*Note:* If you're visiting an art class, make sure the lesson for the day is G-rated and make sure to follow insurance and district policies. *Parental Permission Slips* and *Teacher Permission Slips* given to the students should be signed and returned to the leader before the day of the field trip.

Activity:

Tell the students that the campus visit will include eating lunch in the Student Union, shopping at the bookstore, and visiting a class.

Walk around the campus and talk about what will be expected of the students in junior high and high school.

Talk about your college experience.

Stress the importance of obeying rules and completing homework if the students hope to attend college.

Conclusion:

After the visit, ask if the students still feel college is foreseeable in their future. If so, have them relate what they learned they must do in order to go to college.

(*Note:* These students need to have something to look forward to and something to shoot for. This activity is a way to make college real to them.)

PARENTAL PERMISSION SLIP

I give my permission for my child, ______________________________ ,

to attend ____

on ________/________/____________.

I understand the transportation will be __________________________ .

Signed ______________________________
PARENT OR GUARDIAN

PARENTAL PERMISSION SLIP

I give my permission for my child, ______________________________ ,

to attend ____

on ________/________/____________.

I understand the transportation will be __________________________ .

Signed ______________________________
PARENT OR GUARDIAN

TEACHER PERMISSION SLIP

I give my permission for the counselor to take ______________________________

to attend ____

on _____/_____/__________.

The student must complete all missed assignments by _____/_____/__________.

Signed ____
TEACHER

TEACHER PERMISSION SLIP

I give my permission for the counselor to take ______________________________

to attend ____

on _____/_____/__________.

The student must complete all missed assignments by _____/_____/__________.

Signed ____
TEACHER

HITTING HUMANS

Purpose:

To have the student exhibit nonviolent behavior

Suggested Students:

Students referred because they have behavior problems or have hurt others

Grades K–6

Materials Needed:

For The Leader:

- ☐ Encyclopedia with transparent overlays to show the organs of the human body

For The Student:

- ☐ Copy of *Body Outline* (page 232)
- ☐ Pencil

Activity:

Choose a quiet placc to work with the encyclopedia. Sit next to the student.

Turning to the transparent overlays, explain that even though the skin covers the organs, hitting another person may cause damage that cannot be repaired. The body tries to protect itself by covering the heart and lungs with the rib cage, but hitting can still be dangerous.

If the student is old enough that discussing different body parts is appropriate, select a body part and discuss what irreparable damage could be done to it. Do this with as many body parts as appropriate.

Then ask:

> ***How do you think a person would feel if he or she damaged someone permanently?***
>
> ***How would you feel if you damaged someone permanently?***

Discuss what the student could do instead of hitting.

Give the student a copy of *Body Outline* and a pencil. Have him/her draw a brain in the head of the body outline and fists at the end of the arms. Tell the student to circle the brain as something that might be used and cross out the fists as body parts he/she would not use.

Conclusion:

Tell the student that since people don't usually know what organs they may damage when hitting someone, it's better to use their brain, talk with the person about the situation, and resolve the conflict peacefully.

BODY
OUTLINE

FIRE DRILL FEARS

Purpose:

To teach students to remain calm during a fire drill

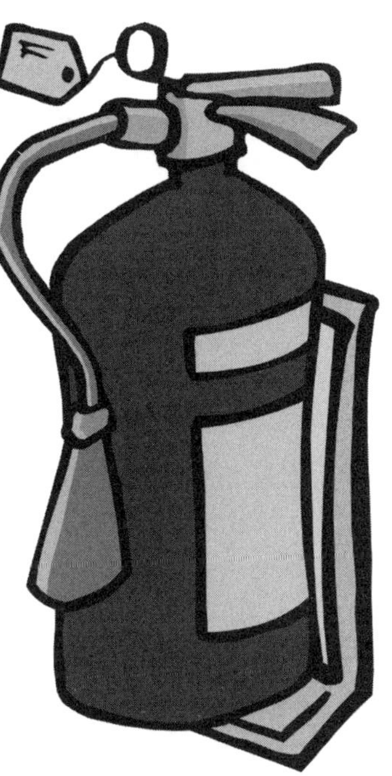

Suggested Students:

Students referred due to high anxiety or panic attacks during fire drills

Grades K–4

Materials Needed:

For The Leader:
- ☐ List of times and dates for fire drills
- ☐ Optional: *Thunder Cake* by Patricia Pollacco

For Each Student:
- ☐ Plastic grocery bag
- ☐ Plastic gloves (Be sure the students are not allergic to latex or other plastic.)

Activity:

Select a large grassy area at the far end of the playground. Have the secretary warn you 10 minutes before the fire alarm will sound.

Go to the selected classrooms and collect three or four students you have seen individually who are terrified by the fire alarm.

While walking to the yard, have the students talk openly about their fears. Some students like to talk about their fears. Tell the students a fire drill is just practice so everyone knows what to do in case of a real fire. Say:

- We have a fire drill a once a month.
- A fire drill does not mean there is a real fire.
- A fire drill is practice so we all know what to do in case there is a fire.

Tell the students that for the _____ years you have been a counselor at the school, there has never been a fire.

Then discuss the following:

> ***What would happen if it were a fire? The sprinklers would spray water before any fire started. They spray water when they sense smoke. There are sprinklers in every room.***
>
> ***Does the sound of the fire alarm bother you? What does it sound like? Some kids say it sounds like a loud duck. That's funny! The fire alarm is a loud, funny sound.***
>
> ***Can the sound hurt you?***
>
> ***When I'm afraid, I sometimes like to think about something different. Let's pick up trash while we wait for the alarm to sound. Let's see who can find the most trash.***

Give each student a trash bag and plastic gloves and have the students pick up trash until the "all clear" signal sounds.

Return to the counselor's office when the all clear signal sounds.

Optional: Read *Thunder Cake* by Patricia Pollacco to remind the students that it isn't unusual to be afraid of something. The little girl in the story is afraid of thunder. It's loud like the fire alarm, but thunder can't hurt us, either.

Discuss ways to overcome fear (think of something else, listen to music, etc.).

Discuss ways to make the sound softer (fingers in ears, sing a song in your mind, self-talk, etc.).

Conclusion:

Have the students develop a plan for the next three fire drills. Begin with what will happen next month when the fire drill occurs. Remind the students that their goal is to walk out with the class before the end of the school year. Ask how much or how little help they think they'll need next month. (Some students like to go with the custodian to pull the alarm, but some are scared to do that.)

LUCKY LIST

Purpose:

To help the student who is down remember what he/she has

Suggested Students:

Students referred as a result of grief, divorce, worry, sadness, change, etc.

Grades K–6

Materials Needed:

For The Leader:

- ☐ 10 or more pages of drawing paper or lined paper
- ☐ Plastic binding

For The Student:

- ☐ Crayons or markers

Preparation:

Using the paper and plastic binding, make a booklet for the student. The student's age will determine how many pages you want to include.

Activity:

Discuss ways to overcome fear (think of something else, listen to music, etc.).

Have the student name all the things that make him/her lucky. Students love this simple concept.

Give the student the booklet and crayons or markers. Title it or have the student title it __________*'s Lucky List.* Tell the student to draw or list all the things that make him/her lucky.

Each time the student comes to the counselor's office, he/she adds more things to the list. The student always leaves the office a little happier because he/she feels lucky. If the student cannot think of anything, prompt him/her with suggestions like:

- Did you sleep in a warm bed last night?
- Did you eat a school breakfast?
- Did someone who loves you buy you that shirt?

Problems that seem insurmountable can be put into perspective when the student reviews the *Lucky List.* For example:

- You have a brother? Lucky!
- You got an *A* on that spelling test? Lucky!

Conclusion:

The student may take the completed booklet home as a reminder of the lucky things he/she has in life.

LIFESTYLE CHANGES

Purpose:

To have the student deal with changes that occur before and during divorce

Suggested Students:

Students referred because of their parents' divorce

Grades K–6

Materials Needed:

For The Leader:
- ☐ Stapler and staples

For The Student:
- ☐ 6 sheets of construction paper of one color and 6 sheets of another color
- ☐ White drawing paper
- ☐ Crayons or markers
- ☐ Glue or glue stick

Activity:

Give the drawing paper, construction paper, glue, and crayons or markers to the student.

Tell the student he/she is going to make a booklet. Explain that one color of construction paper will be for things the student has at his/her dad's house and the other color will be for things the student has at his/her mom's house.

Have the student draw a picture of his/her mother's house on one piece of drawing paper and a picture of his/her father's house on another piece of drawing paper, then glue each drawing to a piece of construction paper.

Have the student name some things he/she has at both houses, draw pictures of these things, explain what was drawn by titling the page, and glue the pages to construction paper of the correct color.

Conclusion:

Staple the completed book together. Allow the student to take it home to share.

CHECKBOOK CHECKUP

Purpose:

To help the student feel comfortable about coming to school

Suggested Students:

Students referred because of school refusal, separation anxiety, or school phobia

Grades K–6

Materials Needed:

For The Leader:

- ☐ Small prizes or certificates for free time (shoot hoops with the counselor for 10 minutes, work on an art project, play a game etc.)
- ☐ Free student checkbooks from a bank or check-printing company (Checks usually come in a box of 100.)

For The Student:

- ☐ A safe place to keep the checkbook

Activity:

Tell the student that kids usually feel better about school if they simply come to school and that you would like him/her to try it and see if it's true. Then ask:

> ***Are you willing to try to begin each morning with fewer tears and tummy aches? If so, I'll give you a checkbook and explain the rules.*** (*Note:* I've never had a child refuse the checkbook.)

Give the child a checkbook and say:

> ***Each morning after the flag salute, if you haven't cried or been sick, you may take your checkbook to your teacher. Your teacher will enter the amount of $1.00 in the check register.***
>
> ***After five days, you may write a check to the counselor for $5.00 and buy a prize.*** (Each prize or coupon should cost $5.00, but most are worth about a quarter.)

Deduct $5.00 from the student's check register. Tell the student he/she may again start earning $1.00 for each day he/she comes to school without tears or illness. (*Note:* I've found it takes less than three weeks for a child come to school without any problems.)

Conclusion:

Talk with the child about how much better he/she feels about coming to school. After the student and leader agree everyone feels better, allow the student to take the checkbook home.

ASCA STANDARDS, COMPETENCIES, AND INDICATORS FOR INDIVIDUAL COUNSELING LESSONS

ACADEMIC DEVELOPMENT

Standard A: Students will acquire the attitudes, knowledge and skills that contribute to effective learning in school and across the life span.

A:A1 Improve Academic Self-concept
A:A1.1 Articulate feelings of competence and confidence as learners
A:A1.2 Display a positive interest in learning
A:A1.3 Take pride in work and achievement
A:A1.4 Accept mistakes as essential to the learning process
A:A1.5 Identify attitudes and behaviors that lead to successful learning

A:A2 Acquire Skills for Improving Learning
A:A2.1 Apply time-management and task-management skills
▶ GETTING ORGANIZED page 144
▶ STAYING ON TASK page 164
A:A2.2 Demonstrate how effort and persistence positively affect learning
▶ STAYING ON TASK page 164
A:A2.3 Use communications skills to know when and how to ask for help when needed
A:A2.4 Apply knowledge and learning styles to positively influence school performance
▶ PREPARE FOR TESTING DAY page 16

A:A3 Achieve School Success
A:A3.1 Take responsibility for their actions
A:A3.2 Demonstrate the ability to work independently, as well as the ability to work cooperatively with other students
A:A3.3 Develop a broad range of interests and abilities
A:A3.4 Demonstrate dependability, productivity and initiative
▶ GETTING ORGANIZED page 144
▶ STAYING ON TASK page 164
A:A3.5 Share knowledge

Standard B: Students will complete school with the academic preparation essential to choose from a wide range of substantial post- secondary options, including college.

A:B1 Improve Learning
A:B1.1 Demonstrate the motivation to achieve individual potential
A:B1.2 Learn and apply critical-thinking skills
A:B1.3 Apply the study skills necessary for academic success at each level
A:B1.4 Seek information and support from faculty, staff, family and peers
A:B1.5 Organize and apply academic information from a variety of sources
A:B1.6 Use knowledge of learning styles to positively influence school performance
A:B1.7 Become a self-directed and independent learner

A:B2 Plan To Achieve Goals
A:B2.1 Establish challenging academic goals in elementary, middle/jr. high and high school
A:B2.2 Use assessment results in educational planning
A:B2.3 Develop and implement annual plan of study to maximize academic ability and achievement
A:B2.4 Apply knowledge of aptitudes and interests to goal setting
A:B2.5 Use problem-solving and decision-making skills to assess progress toward educational goals

A:B2.6 Understand the relationship between classroom performance and success in school
▶STAYING ON TASK page 164
A:B2.7 Identify post-secondary options consistent with interests, achievement, aptitude and abilities

Standard C: Students will understand the relationship of academics to the world of work and to life at home and in the community.

A:C1 Relate School To Life Experiences
A:C1.1 Demonstrate the ability to balance school, studies, extracurricular activities, leisure time and family life
A:C1.2 Seek co-curricular and community experiences to enhance the school experience
A:C1.3 Understand the relationship between learning and work
A:C1.4 Demonstrate an understanding of the value of lifelong learning as essential to seeking, obtaining and maintaining life goals
A:C1.5 Understand that school success is the preparation to make the transition from student to community member
A:C1.6 Understand how school success and academic achievement enhance future career and vocational opportunities
▶FIELD TRIP page 226

CAREER DEVELOPMENT

Standard A: Students will acquire the skills to investigate the world of work in relation to knowledge of self and to make informed career decisions.

C:A1 Develop Career Awareness
C:A1.1 Develop skills to locate, evaluate and interpret career information
C:A1.2 Learn about the variety of traditional and nontraditional occupations
C:A1.3. Develop an awareness of personal abilities, skills, interests and motivations
C:A1.4 Learn how to interact and work cooperatively in teams
C:A1.5 Learn to make decisions
C:A1.6 Learn how to set goals
C:A1.7 Understand the importance of planning
C:A1.8 Pursue and develop competency in areas of interest
C:A1.9 Develop hobbies and vocational interests
C:A1.10 Balance between work and leisure time

C:A2 Develop Employment Readiness
C:A2.1 Acquire employability skills such as working on a team, problem-solving and organizational skills
C:A2.2 Apply job readiness skills to seek employment opportunities
C:A2.3 Demonstrate knowledge about the changing workplace
C:A2.4 Learn about the rights and responsibilities of employers and employees
C:A2.5 Learn to respect individual uniqueness in the workplace
C:A2.6 Learn how to write a resume
C:A2.7 Develop a positive attitude toward work and learning
C:A2.8 Understand the importance of responsibility, dependability, punctuality, integrity and effort in the workplace
C:A2.9 Utilize time- and task-management skills

Standard B: Students will employ strategies to achieve future career goals with success and satisfaction.

C:B1 Acquire Career Information
C:B1.1 Apply decision-making skills to career planning, course selection and career transition
C:B1.2 Identify personal skills, interests and abilities and relate them to current career choice
C:B1.3 Demonstrate knowledge of the career-planning process
C:B1.4 Know the various ways in which occupations can be classified
C:B1.5 Use research and information resources to obtain career information
C:B1.6 Learn to use the Internet to access career-planning information

C:B1.7 Describe traditional and nontraditional career choices and how they relate to career choice
C:B1.8 Understand how changing economic and societal needs influence employment trends and future training
C:B2 Identify Career Goals
C:B2.1 Demonstrate awareness of the education and training needed to achieve career goals
C:B2.2 Assess and modify their educational plan to support career
C:B2.3 Use employability and job readiness skills in internship, mentoring, shadowing and/or other work experience
C:B2.4 Select course work that is related to career interests
C:B2.5 Maintain a career-planning portfolio

Standard C: Students will understand the relationship between personal qualities, education, training and the world of work.

C:C1 Acquire Knowledge to Achieve Career Goals
C:C1.1 Understand the relationship between educational achievement and career success
C:C1.2 Explain how work can help to achieve personal success and satisfaction
C:C1.3 Identify personal preferences and interests influencing career choice and success
C:C1.4 Understand that the changing workplace requires lifelong learning and acquiring new skills
C:C1.5 Describe the effect of work on lifestyle
C:C1.6 Understand the importance of equity and access in career choice
C:C1.7 Understand that work is an important and satisfying means of personal expression

C:C2 Apply Skills to Achieve Career Goals
C:C2.1 Demonstrate how interests, abilities and achievement relate to achieving personal, social, educational and career goals
C:C2.2 Learn how to use conflict management skills with peers and adults
C:C2.3 Learn to work cooperatively with others as a team member
C:C2.4 Apply academic and employment readiness skills in workbased learning situations such as internships, shadowing and/or mentoring experiences

PERSONAL/SOCIAL DEVELOPMENT

Standard A: Students will acquire the knowledge, attitudes and interpersonal skills to help them understand and respect self and others.

PS:A1 Acquire Self-Knowledge
PS:A1.1 Develop positive attitudes toward self as a unique and worthy person
- ▶FRIENDSHIP—I AM NOT YOUR PUPPET page 20
- ▶ELIMINATING SELF-DESTRUCTIVE BEHAVIORS page 41
- ▶COPING WITH BODY IMAGES page 44
- ▶SELF-ESTEEM/POSITIVE AFFIRMATIONS page 52
- ▶I NOSE I'M SPECIAL page 103
- ▶SOME BUNNY page 115
- ▶PERSONAL PORTFOLIO page 122
- ▶JUST ME! BOX page 210
- ▶MY FEELINGS/THOUGHTS DIARY page 212
- ▶POSITIVE THOUGHTS DIARY page 216
- ▶LUCKY LIST page 235

PS:A1.2 Identify values, attitudes and beliefs
- ▶KEEP YOUR WORD page 25
- ▶FRIENDSHIP SHOULDN'T HURT page 31
- ▶HANDS OFF MY STUFF page 38
- ▶COPING WITH BODY IMAGES page 44
- ▶INITIAL INTERVIEW page 82
- ▶MAKING FRIENDS page 95
- ▶DIVORCE—FUN THINGS I DO WITH MY MOM AND DAD page 99

PS:A2 Acquire Interpersonal Skills

PS:A2.1 Recognize that everyone has rights and responsibilities

PS:A2.2 Respect alternative points of view

PS:A2.3 Recognize, accept, respect and appreciate individual differences

PS:A2.4 Recognize, accept and appreciate ethnic and cultural diversity

PS:A2.5 Recognize and respect differences in various family configurations

PS:A2.6 Use effective communications skills

PS:A2.7 Know that communication involves speaking, listening and nonverbal behavior

PS:A2.8 Learn how to make and keep friends

Standard B: Students will make decisions, set goals and take necessary action to achieve goals.

PS:B1 Self-Knowledge Application

PS:B1.1 Use a decision-making and problem-solving model

Standard C: Students will understand safety and survival skills.

PS:C1 Acquire Personal Safety Skills

PS:C1.1 Demonstrate knowledge of personal information (i.e., telephone number, home address, emergency contact)

PS:C1.2 Learn about the relationship between rules, laws, safety and the protection of rights of the individual

PS:C1.3 Learn about the differences between appropriate and inappropriate physical contact

PS:C1.4 Demonstrate the ability to set boundaries, rights and personal privacy

PS:C1.5 Differentiate between situations requiring peer support and situations requiring adult professional help

PS:C1.6 Identify resource people in the school and community, and know how to seek their help

PS:C1.7 Apply effective problem-solving and decision-making skills to make safe and healthy choices

PS:C1.8 Learn about the emotional and physical dangers of substance use and abuse

PS:C1.9 Learn how to cope with peer pressure

PS:C1.10 Learn techniques for managing stress and conflict

PS:C1.11 Learn coping skills for managing life events